COMMUNITY COLLABORATIONS FOR FAMILY LITERACY HANDBOOK

SHELLEY QUEZADA
RUTH S. NICKSE

NEAL-SCHUMAN PUBLISHERS, INC.
NEW YORK   LONDON

Published by Neal-Schuman Publishers, Inc.
100 Varick Street
New York, NY 10013

Printed and bound in the United States of America

Library of Congress Cataloging-in-Publication Data

Quezada, Shelley.
    Community collaborations for family literacy handbook / Shelley
Quezada. Ruth S. Nickse.
        p.   cm.
    Includes bibliographical references (p.) and index.
    ISBN 1-55570-164-7
    1. Libraries and new literates--United States. 2. Family literacy
programs United Stats. 3. Public libraries--United States-
-Services to the illiterate. 4. Libraries and community--United
States.   I. Nickse, Ruth S. II. Title.
Z716.45.Q49 1993
027.6--dc20   93-21017
                                           CIP

To our colleagues in adult literacy,
libraries, human and child services
who believed that a family literacy program
could make a difference
in their communities.

CONTENTS

INTRODUCTION

One of the earliest experiments in a family reading project was *Collaborations for Literacy (CFL)* which was originated at Boston University and conducted from 1984 to 1989. A collaboration with the public library presented the initial opportunity for Ruth Nickse to work with Shelley Quezada, literacy consultant for the Massachusetts Board of Library Commissioners (MBLC), the State Library agency. The project, conceived and designed by Ruth Nickse, went through various changes as it refined the family literacy concept. Each new phase of the project revealed the complexities and difficulties of organizing a family reading intervention/illiteracy prevention program although each phase also seemed to confirm the intuitive appeal of this instructional approach.

Early experiences with this evolving program brought these authors face-to-face with the need for collaboration among libraries, adult education programs, schoolbased programs, and others in the community with an interest and a concern about literacy. They felt compelled to embark on a complicated process that involved coordination and joint planning across organizational mandates and habits; a new process for most human service workers. This process proved to be rewarding because services jointly planned and provided involve the community in raising literacy achievement. The five-year relationship of the authors with this seminal family literacy project prompted the development of the Community Collaborations for Family Literacy (CCFL) project (see Appendix A).

This *Community Collaborations for Family Literacy Handbook* is an outcome of the collective experience of six communities in Massachusetts which participated in a 16-month project to develop collaborative strategies to implement a plan for family literacy. The Massachusetts Board of Library Commissioners, the state library agency, received a LSCA Title VI grant from the U.S. Depart ment of Education to develop the project. This 16-month study involved a total of more than 40 leaders in six cities who represented various social and educational services participating in a jointly developed project. The purpose was to improve the ability of public libraries to serve the needs of at-risk families by planning for the development of a family literacy program suited to each community. It was hoped that this project would result in a viable community effort and at the same time enable others to learn from the experience.

Each local library coordinated a team of representatives from basic adult education, Chapter One programs, and family support services. Each of the six community teams, which varied in size and composition, held a series of planning meetings during a nine month period and were invited at the end of that time to submit a letter of intent to compete for federal funds administered by the state library agency.

Members of the local teams, who had little or no prior experience with collaborative planning for community services delivery, were aided by the project staff in several ways. These included: information sharing and access including a special, invitational, state-wide family literacy conference; site visits by staff to each community; provision of new books, research articles, and program materials on family literacy to each library; and special mailings and ongoing technical assistance.

Community teams took responsibility for keeping track of their planning efforts by documenting meetings, the barriers faced, solutions adopted to enhance collaboration, and other evidence of their working together. These collective notes became the basis for the case studies which are explored in Appendix A of this Handbook. Methods of data collection included:

- Review of site notebook.
- Evaluations of conferences and workshops.
- In-depth interviews with participants.
- Site visit notes.
- An evaluation workshop.

Results of the project include:

- A unique, new, and positive experience in community planning for the majority of participants.
- The use of the collaborative community development process which resulted in five proposals for LSCA Title I funding.
- Successful submission by one community for an *Even Start* grant.
- Submission of two proposals to LSCA Title VI (Federal Library Literacy program).
- Publication of the Handbook which records the joint planning process in each community.

Participants agreed that this project created an unusual opportunity for local networking and planning within a supportive frame-work which increased their knowledge of family literacy, reduced isolation and overlapping services, changed their conception of service from a focus on individuals to a focus on families, inspired them to plan collaboratively for family literacy programs resulting in successful proposals which earned funding for several communities to date.

Partly due to the response generated by this project, the State Bureau of Adult Education has identified family literacy as a priority and has assigned an educational consultant to develop programs and provide services. Furthermore, conference participants from a broad range of adult education, library, family, and school programs indicated that they would pursue further funding for initiating family literacy projects in their communities as a result of their attendance at the state-wide conference. Within the library community alone, 18 public libraries applied for LSCA Title I funding in FY91 as a result of their participation in the conference. Lastly, the project promoted the introduction of a new statewide policy initiative in family literacy within the Governor's Education Reform Bill.

This handbook evolved because the experience with the CCFL project was successful. It helped the community teams to gain knowledge and techniques that better utilized collaborative modes to their advantage. The authors gained knowledge about the structure and operation of collaborations which they hope will be as useful to others.

The *Community Collaborations for Family Literacy Handbook* is divided into three major sections. The first provides an overview of the history of family literacy with background information to provide a justification for family literacy programs. The second section contains specific suggestions for practical steps in convening a cross-section of community providers to develop a shared plan for specific family programs. The third section details a step-by-step process which will help the reader to write a successful family literacy proposal. An in-depth study of the Massachusetts Community Collaborations for Family Literacy Model, which was the inspiration and basis for this handbook, is located in Appendix A. The information contained in the case study may be especially useful to state level adult education, along with library and human service providers in the design of their statewide efforts to initiate family literacy proposals.

SECTION ONE

1
INTRODUCTION AND NATIONAL BACKGROUND

According to Marian Wright Edelman, Executive Director of the Children's Defense Fund, 33 million people (one-seventh of all Americans including 13 million children) are now poor as a result of economic recession, structural changes in the economy, stagnated wages, and federal tax and budget policies.

Former Secretary of Education William Bennett states in his introduction to *First Lessons* that by the time children in the kindergarten class of 2010 reach their 18th birthdays, only 41 out of 100 will be living in traditional family units.

It is estimated that one out of five American children are living in poverty, including one of four children under the age of six. Poverty poses a risk for malnutrition, child abuse, educational disability, low achievement, increased school drop out rates, and crime. These facts are compounded by changes in family structure due to high rates of divorce, separation, and teenage pregnancy. These factors present new challenges to those who work with families. An increasing number of working and single parents must maintain their preschool children in some kind of child care facility which may be inadequate or makeshift. As these children get older, many become latchkey children who must fend for themselves on the streets or be at home alone. When adults return, children often find themselves in a non-supportive atmosphere where neither nutritional nor emotional needs are met by parents barely able to cope with survival problems.

For most adults and their children designated "at risk," survival is the most critical problem—one which they face on a daily basis. Lack of adequate food, housing, and counseling services have locked many into a cycle of hopelessness and poverty. They need information on health care for themselves and their children, employment, housing, parenting, and substance abuse counseling. Without the educational skills to understand and process it, this information is meaningless to them. These parents need to improve their basic and functional skills in order to meet their personal individual goals as family members, parents, consumers, and citizens.

Family literacy is an emerging discipline in adult education which focuses on improving the basic literacy level of an adult which will impact the literacy level of the child for whom that adult is responsible. Programs are currently taking place in early childhood education centers, school-based Chapter One (ESEA) programs, adult basic education programs, libraries, the workplace, bilingual education programs, and privately or corporately funded centers.

Although family literacy programs use a variety of approaches, they share some of the following characteristics:

- Programs target individuals who are family members in need of basic skills, particularly literacy development.
- Program design is conceptualized around the needs of the individual as part of a family unit. Thus, it includes information such as parenting, handling stress, money management, children's schooling, and other functional content.
- Literacy, pre-literacy, and developmentally appropriate activities for children are frequently included as a program component.
- Quality program development is based on a community needs assessment and increasingly reflects a collaboration based on the complex nature of how families work. Therefore, programs necessitate forming partnerships between those providing services to adults as well as to children.

National Movement Toward Collaborative Projects

Traditionally, the human service needs of adults and children have been met by a virtual army of workers employed by diverse agencies and organizations. For the most part these efforts have been parallel but separate. Childcare and social workers, early childhood and adult basic education teachers, librarians, as well as welfare and family support workers and policy makers at the local, state, and national level have all concerned themselves with the needs of disadvantaged children and adults. Despite large investments of resources, fragmented systems frequently fail the families involved.

Many services are crisis-oriented, rather than preventive—designed to address problems which have already occurred. The current system of social welfare and education divides the problems of families into distinct and rigid categories, failing to reflect their interrelated causes and solutions, as well as their intergenerational nature. Poor communication among the myriad public and private agencies and a system of turf protection prevents active collaboration, although the general missions of the agencies are similar and the target population often the same families. Agencies, while employing well-trained professionals, simply do not have the expertise in the multiple areas needed to provide comprehensive services. A new paradigm is needed.

Models of human service delivery are being developed which involve structuring interagency partnerships and collaborations to connect children and adults to more comprehensive services. For example, the Robert Wood Johnson Foundation has funded five programs which represent a collaboration among county health and social services providing food stamps and education programs to serve targeted families. This approach is emerging as a key ingredient of family literacy programs. One of the earliest family literacy programs was deliberately named "Collaborations for Literacy" to accurately describe this structure and recognize its interagency partnerships.

Acknowledging the need to work in cooperative arrangements is a necessary first step that acknowledges participation in a collaborative partnership as a new method of working together that must be learned through practice. Collaborations are dynamic, often difficult to organize and maintain, yet well worth the effort.

Partnerships have the potential to provide better organized and effective services and perhaps will eventually lower the costs of human services. Sometimes partnerships are unnecessarily thrown together in funding proposals with little regard for the actual steps involved in developing successful projects.

When too little time is spent on planning and working out issues, otherwise well-meaning coalitions may experience frustration which can create unpleasant and difficult relationships. Collaborations, however, are gaining credence even at the federal level and the recent attention to the National Educational Goals provides a context for meaningful collaboration to begin.

The passage of the National Literacy Act (July, 1991) acknowledges the value of collaborative efforts by encouraging each state to set up an Advisory Council on Adult Education and Literacy to include a representative cross section from public education, workforce, human service agencies, and libraries.

THE NATIONAL LITERACY ACT OF 1991

Quoting Thomas Jefferson, who declared, "A nation that expects to be ignorant and free expects what never was and never will be," President George Bush signed the National Literacy Act of 1991 into law on July 25, 1991. The National Literacy Act represents the most comprehensive and serious legislation pertaining to the literacy needs of adults in this country who lack the basic skills of reading, writing, computation, and oral communication. It has implications for libraries, the workforce, and adult, early childhood, and secondary education. It encourages the development of demonstration literacy projects in prisons and pays significant attention to a growing need to address the literacy needs of adults and children in a family context.

Highlights of the Bill Include:

- The establishment of a National Institute for Literacy to coordinate federal literacy programs and conduct research into programs and issues.

- A grant program to establish State Literacy Resource Centers to provide training and coordination of federal, state, and local programs.
- Aid to set up a National Workforce Literacy Assistance Collaborative to assist small- and medium-size businesses to develop literacy programs.
- The expansion of Even Start from a federal to a state program as the Even Start Family Literacy program.
- Opportunities to expand Workplace Literacy Partnerships.
- Continued support of the Vista Volunteers for Literacy program.
- Moneys to establish competitive "Gateway Grants" for public housing authorities' literacy programs.
- The inclusion of a discretionary grants program to states for demonstration literacy projects for the incarcerated.

The changes which may have the most relevance to libraries and the community agencies with which they work are changes in the language of this State Basic Grant program under the Adult Education Act which requires that states provide direct and equitable access to Federal adult education funds by LEAS (Local Education Associations), public or private nonprofit agencies, community-based organizations, agencies responsible for corrections education, post secondary educational institutions, and those which serve educationally disadvantaged adults.

The 1991 National Literacy Act also provides two million dollars each year for the next four years to fund the Corporation for Public Broadcasting to develop Family Literacy Public Broadcasting. Designation of these funds in a federal program shows recognition of the power of the media to motivate parents to have greater involvement in the literacy development of their children. *Project Literacy US (PLUS)* began highlighting family literacy as one of its top priorities, recognizing that a love of reading must be fostered in the family if it is to flourish in the schoolroom.

The National Literacy Act acknowledges the value of collaborative efforts by encouraging each state to set up an Advisory Council on Adult Education and Literacy to include a representative cross section from public education, workforce, human service agencies, and libraries.

The National Educational goals described below promote family literacy and provide a context in which collaborations can get started.

THE NATIONAL EDUCATIONAL GOALS

The moneys earmarked to support the adult and family literacy in the National Literacy Act must be considered in relation to the major reforms which are being proposed for the American educational system. In 1990, President Bush and the nation's governors convened an educational summit and formulated six national goals to be reached by the turn of the century. The two goals which speak most directly to the issue of family literacy are:

Goal One: All children in America will start school ready to learn.

Goal Five: Every Adult will be literate and will possess the knowledge and skills necessary to compete in a global economy and exercise the rights and responsibilities of citizenship.

These goals are totally interconnected and basically unachievable if not examined as two halves of a larger issue. If, as a nation, we are truly serious about meeting the educational needs of our children, this can best be accomplished by addressing the literacy needs of their parents.

Early research indicates that providing support for family literacy is the soundest and most effective way to move a set of educational goals beyond the platitudes and hopeful statements about school reform into the reality of the American family unit. Only at the family level can we ultimately break the widening cycle of intergenerational illiteracy.

Family and Intergenerational Literacy Programs

The concept of family and intergenerational literacy emerged in practice in several early demonstration projects held in 1984 that focused on adults in this country who lacked the basic skills of reading, writing, computation, and oral communication. The concept has evolved with implications for libraries, the workforce, and adult, early childhood, and secondary education. It proliferates rapidly to embrace a wide variety of activities that unite adults and children in literacy improvement efforts. The idea appeals to a broad audience of theorists, program designers, funders, and legislators who find the concept attractive. The improvement of adults' basic skills and those of children from the same intervention combines agendas of mutual importance.

The advantages of a family or intergenerational approach appear to increase motivation for literacy development among both adults and children, along with providing opportunities for closeness and shared activities—in short, the joy of reading. To date, there is little rigorous evidence using well controlled studies that may confirm these expectations. Early research findings (Nickse, Askov) appear generally promising and major research efforts are currently underway to test this hypothesis.

For example, the national evaluation of the Even Start intergenerational programs should provide some concrete data from across the nation on the effectiveness of certain types of family literacy programs. The results of this study will be delivered to Congress by the U. S. Department of Education in 1993. This study describes more than 150 demonstration programs serving several thousands of low literate families with children ranging in age from newborn to seven years old who are eligible for family literacy services, and examines the effects of participation on them.

While results of objective and controlled studies aimed at proving the merit of the idea are awaited, examples of practice deemed successful by both participants and staffs involved in programs abound, and seem to confirm positive results. Parents and adults reading to and with children are having fun enjoying a new relationship and, it is hoped, improving a range of literacy skills and behaviors. Initial evaluation of national Even Start programs show that collaboration is a key element in successful programs.

FAMILY LITERACY PROGRAM TYPES

The seminal work on family literacy is Ruth S. Nickse's excellent monograph *Family and Intergenerational Literacy Programs: An Update of the "Noises of Literacy."* In her study of family literacy programs, Nickse has classified family literacy programs based on two factors:

1. The target group which receives the service (e.g. either parent, or child).
2. The method of intervention.

The following typology includes features and concerns for four generic types of programs:

Type 1: Direct Adults-Direct Children
Type 2: Indirect Adults-Indirect Children
Type 3: Direct Adults-Indirect Children
Type 4: Direct Children-Indirect Adults

The Typology (Figure 1.1.) helps to distinguish one type from the other. A typology is useful for practitioners, researchers, and policy makers. It helps in planning programs, in discussing them, and in training staff. Its use enables a clearer picture of available community services for literacy development, helps to increase collaboration, and reduces redundancy in service. Typology has proved useful in identifying critical differences between program types while also defining program goals and expectations, thus becoming an aid in planning for their design, administration, and evaluation.

A longer, evaluative discussion of these four generic types of family literacy programs is found in Nickse's text which is available through the ERIC Clearinghouse at Ohio State University.

THE RESEARCH BACKGROUND: THE IMPORTANCE OF STORY BOOK READING

The goal of a family literacy program is to enhance the lives of parents and children through the joy of reading, and not incidentally, to also improve the literacy skills, attitudes, values, and behaviors of both. Evidence from adult basic education, early childhood education, cognitive science, emergent literacy, and family systems theory all supports the importance of adults in children's early literacy development. Sharing books in families, when appropriately undertaken,

FIGURE 1.1. Four Generic Types of Family and Intergenerational Literacy Programs

TYPE	Examples of Features	Examples of Concerns and Issues
TYPE 1 Parent/Child	Goal is positive, long term family intervention • parent/child; parent; child; activities • intense, frequent participation • highly structured; formal instruction • direct instruction; dual curriculum • ECE/ABE staff team • monitored attendance • dedicated site • long term intervention	• long term program • high time commitment necessary • retention in program is a problem • facilities for ECE/ABE together • transportation for families • child care for infants, toddlers • high degree of collaboration needed • substantial costs to initiate and maintain; funding an issue
TYPE 2 Adult/Child	Goal is supplementary, for skill building and enjoyment • non-related adults and children; parents and children • lower level of intensity, participation • less structured; more informal • weekends, after school programs • collaborations (none to many) • adapted sites • short term intervention	• little or no formal, sustained literacy instruction for adult/child • less intensive participation • lacks full time ECE/ABE staff • less parent/child interaction • parttime staffing • short term programs • costs to initiate and maintain; funding an issue
TYPE 3 Adult Alone	Goal is parent education • parents/adults alone – children present infrequently or not at all • workshop formats; low intensity • peer instruction and practice • "portable" curriculum • parent networking • short term intervention	• short term program • no supervised parent/child interaction • parttime staffing; consultants • parent reports of programs' success • developmentally inappropriate activities may be used by parents • costs to initiate and maintain; funding an issue
TYPE 4 Child Alone	Goal is supplementary school related literacy improvement for children • school-based children; at-home parents • school linked program • teacher supervised • take-home materials for children • short term intervention	• short term program • parents receive no literacy instruction for themselves • parent may not provide support at home for child • parent may not participate in workshops, rallies • low cost

Adapted from: © Nickse, R. A Typology of Family and Intergenerational Literacy Programs: Implications for Evaluation, 1991. (ERIC ED 333 166)

sets a pattern for talking together about things and ideas and adds to the pleasure of each other's company. Through shared activities, the social uses of literacy are incorporated along with orientations to concepts about books and print materials, and the cognitive tasks of asking and answering questions which are so important to the children's school success. The development of concepts about reading and writing at home, before children enter school, is the subject of fascinating studies in an area of reading called emergent literacy.

Many literate homes help to create atmospheres where parents act as reading and writing models, and books, newspapers, and magazines are available

---

FIGURE 1.2.

" SLAM, BANG, BOP - the Big Billy Goat Gruff knocks the Troll off the bridge forever, and Little Billy Goat Gruff, Bigger Billy Goat Gruff and Big Billy Goat Gruff safely cross the bridge to the bright green grass. The End."

As the parent reads to the young child both are engrossed, sitting close together, studying the brightly colored pages. Even though the parent reads this simple text with some hesitancy stumbling over the word "Gruff" repeatedly when it appears -the little boy is enthralled, asks questions, points to the Troll's outlandish appearance and to the features - horns, beards, and tails of the three Billy Goats Gruff.

This 23 year -old mother is enjoying a new experience with her son that she herself has never had as a child being read to by an adult. And through this shared and pleasurable experience, the little boy is absorbing basic ideas about reading vital to early school success with reading. He is learning from his (and every child's) first teacher, his mother.

and freely used by both parents and children. By the age of 18 months, many young children in these homes have a grasp of story book concepts and are learning to distinguish the different parts of a book and to understand its use as a positive experience.

However, low literate parents may not, for a variety of reasons, read to and with their children. They may be unaware that reading together helps builds skills, or reading may not be a family or community habit. The parents themselves may be too poor to buy books, or too poorly skilled and embarrassed by their own faulty reading to attempt reading to their children. They may not feel comfortable in their local libraries—perhaps they have never been inside them. It is these parents and primary caretakers that family and intergenerational literacy programs target for assistance.

Design and Implementation

Many communities are beginning to plan for family literacy programs of one type or another. Based on experiences, several challenges in the design consideration, implementation, and evaluation emerge. Programs are frequently service oriented, experimental, and designed more on an instinct that the concept "makes sense" rather than on a firm base backed by research. While programs designed many times "on instinct" alone prove successful, there is merit in learning from the earlier work. Here are some tips.

PROGRAM DESIGN TIPS

- There is much variation in programs because they are locally designed and focus on specific populations, community needs, and available resources. Tailor the program to the community using a needs assessment. (See chapter 5). Programs which serve increasingly multicultural emerging majorities must be designed with sensitivity and experience.
- A multicultural staff is a strong program asset which attracts families. Staff with backgrounds in both adult and early childhood education help make an integrated curriculum, so build in joint staff training.
- Collaborations with local agencies expands the sense of program ownership and increases scarce resources.
- The best designed programs make accommodations for parents who lack adequate transportation and child care. Vouchers, carfare, ride sharing, and the use of school buses and dedicated vans are some solutions to transportation needs. Child care for those children not involved in the programs can be provided on site through arrangements with volunteers, or by the use of vouchers which allow parents to pay sitters when children cannot be accommodated on site.

- Celebrate the richness of the multicultural community by including their cultures in the curriculum and by having representative community members on the program staff.

IMPLEMENTATION TIPS

- These programs are usually complex, so start small. It is easier to enlarge your program based on the track record of a successful program than to start off too big.
- Use materials which are attractive to both adults and children. These are usually books which have themes understood by all ages. Some are suggested in the Resource List at the end of the book.
- Supplement the formal program with a variety of take-home materials. Use special book bags for books, videos, games, and toys.
- Accept the fact that families frequently move around the community. Set up a buddy system to keep them informed about your program.
- Establish a parents' committee to help with the program.
- Realize that many families may not be accustomed to having their children with them during educational events.

EVALUATION TIPS

- Select measures appropriate to the population served and the intensity, duration, and goals of the program.
- Consult measures listed in chapter 5 of this Handbook to help design a useful evaluation for the program's revision and growth.

Five Initiatives

Two of the most notable statewide initiatives have come from the state library agencies of California and New York. In 1990 the Iowa State Library commissioned Debra Wilcox Johnson of the University of Wisconsin/Madison to conduct a national survey of library family literacy programs. Her excellent monograph, *Library Family Literacy Programs,* provides an in-depth overview of the variety of programs and activities taking place within libraries. In recent years, through her work on family literacy evaluation, she has developed some "indicators of success" in family programs which would be useful for those developing or seeking to evaluate a family program. Some of these indicators are discussed in chapter 5.

CALIFORNIA'S FAMILY FOR LITERACY PROGRAM

The California State Library initiated the *Families for Literacy Program* (FFL) in 1988 through a specific state appropriation. The program enabled libraries which were already providing adult literacy services as participants in the state funded California Literacy Campaign to add a family literacy component.

Now in its fifth year, the *Families for Literacy Program* serves an average of 24 libraries in the state. Carole Talan serves as Family Literacy Program Coordinator. With a background in both reading and literacy education, she has made this program an exciting model for library family literacy. Adult learners in the FFL program are introduced to the joy of reading together as a family. Program components include:

- Book ownership—especially important for parents and children who have never owned their own books.
- Use of the library as a site for family meetings—providing an introduction to the resources of the library.
- Use of children's books as a part of the tutoring/learning experience.
- Information on selection and use of books for children.
- Provision of appropriate materials on parenting, child care, health, and nutrition.

Some library programs have developed videos which are designed to raise awareness and engage community agencies in collaboration. The program reaches 683 eligible families and serves 685 children under the age of five. These programs receive funding support from the California State Library with support from a Family Literacy program specialist who provides technical assistance. Several libraries have been able to assume the program costs in the third and fourth year as part of a local responsibility thus freeing funds up for new programs to begin.

This past year, the California State Library contracted with Educational Testing Service in Pasadena, California to conduct an evaluation of the Families for Literacy program and to determine the overall effectiveness of the program design. The key findings and major recommendations are contained in *An Evaluation of California's Families for Literacy Program* (Solarzano and Baca, 1991). Key findings included:

- In the fiscal year 1990-91, more than 8,690 books selected for quality and interest were given away to participating families.
- Storytelling was the most often reported activity during the group sessions.
- Fingerplays, games, songs, and creative dramatics were also employed to develop the listening and attention skills of children and to serve as a model for primary caregivers.
- Most adults participating in the program received one-on-one instruction

from a tutor at least once a week and were introduced to books on parenting, child care, or nutrition. Tutors also assisted parents in selecting books for their children.

- In addition to the more traditional storytelling, programs providing support activities such as crafts, puppets, or singalongs were popular.
- The majority (79%) of adult learners were from minority backgrounds, with Hispanics (47%) and African-Americans as (25%) the greatest number. 70 percent spoke English at home as their primary language.
- The most common recruitment mechanism was through flyers, brochures, and posters. Child care centers, family and social service agencies, and local churches were popular locations for successful parent recruitment.

Nine major recommendations were:

1. To extend the eligibility criteria for Families for Literacy children to eight years old . . . or eliminate the age restriction requirement altogether.
2. Address the academic needs of older siblings.
3. Expand the location of Families for Literacy meetings to include other sites.
4. Expand the communication potential among library services working with the Families for Literacy program.
5. Expand local Families for Literacy programs' communication with child care providers.
6. Continue to allow programs to provide services to families that meet their needs.
7. Revise the Families for Literacy forms (e.g. proposals, mid-year, and final report) to gather additional progress data that are quantifiable and standard across programs. Further, these forms should be aligned so information needed for the California State Library final report can be gathered during the course of the program.
8. Expand the eligibility criteria for parents participating in the FFL.
9. Provide additional funding to programs so they can maintain, solidify, and expand their services to families.

NEW YORK STATE LIBRARY FAMILY LITERACY PROJECT

The New York State Library used LSCA Title I funds in 1987-88 to provide start up grants to seventeen library systems for family reading programs. The New York programs placed its major emphasis on providing resource materials for family-centered activities utilizing the broadest definition of family literacy—involving parents and children together in literacy activities. Although the New York programs served both small rural and large urban public libraries, many libraries provided outreach activities that took place in family shelters, maternity wards, and Well Baby clinics with teenage mothers and with incarcerated youth offenders who were also parents. These programs, like the California programs, called for the development of new relationships among children's librarians, outreach and adult literacy specialists, as well as health and youth agency personnel who were providing a blending of services to a shared target audience.

According to Carol Sheffer, Outreach/Literacy Consultant at the New York State Library, the program served 107 libraries in 52 counties and reached 220,000 children. Many libraries used these funds to develop preschool corners in an area of the children's room. A series of kits were developed including puppets and audiobook cassette packages which were placed in a designated corner of the library. Many parents who had not previously been able to afford these "extras" utilized the preschool corner—complete with crayons, blank paper, and craft materials as an activity center for parents and children. This provided preliteracy materials which are generally lacking in the homes of many families and which literate people usually take for granted.

ALA/BELL ATLANTIC FAMILY LITERACY PROJECT

Now in its fourth year, The American Library Association (ALA) and Bell Atlantic Family Literacy Project is an ambitious joint effort between the Bell-Atlantic Charitable Foundation and the American Library Association. This private/public partnership has provided more than $200,000 over the past two years for collaborative efforts in the Middle Atlantic States region and, in January, 1992 announced a commitment of another $500,000 for project development over the next three years.

In order for libraries to be eligible, they are required to form a partnership with a local Bell company, and an adult education specialist or literacy provider in their community. An important component of the Bell-Atlantic project is a two-day training session for participating teams which is held in a central location in the Middle Atlantic states. The sessions provide team building activities and training for the library, adult literacy and corporate partners in the development of their own family literacy programs. According to Margaret Monsour, ALA/Bell-Atlantic Literacy Project Director, working under ALA's office for Library Outreach Services, grant recipients are also required to provide training to other literacy providers and librarians in their communities. This requirement extends the knowledge and skills which they have acquired through the development of their family literacy projects. This exciting public/private partnership has proved highly successful and should be more widely disseminated within the private sector as a potential model for replication.

A STATEWIDE FAMILY LITERACY INITIATIVE

Since 1989, The Illinois Literacy Resource Development Center (ILRDC) has conducted a study of family literacy programs in Illinois with support from the John D. and Catherine T. MacArthur Foundation, Illinois State Board of Education-

Adult Education and Chicago Tribune Charities. The initial study, *The Mechanics of Success for Families, Family Literacy Report #1,* reviewed nineteen program sites in the state of Illinois.

The focus of this report was on the evaluation *activities* conducted at each of the sites rather than a evaluation of each program. Phase 2 of this project has been an overview of changes at model sites during the course of the second year. The ILRDC worked with evaluation literature in the field of family support and designed an evaluation framework which was documented in *The Mechanics of Success for Families, Report #2.*

In Phase 3 of the project, the ILRDC assisted family literacy providers to integrate the evaluation framework into their programs.

Specific project goals were:

1. Assist local programs to develop and implement evaluation systems.
2. Test the usefulness of the evaluation framework as a tool for local family literacy providers.

The instruments and tools which family literacy sites used reflected the unique nature of each specific program. All process and data synthesis was done by the ILRDC and the results were published in, *Fine Tuning the Mechanics of Success for Families, Report #3.*

Now in its final phase, the ILRDC has brought together key stake-holders to develop a list of needs and policy recommendations for those interested in advancing family literacy opportunities in Illinois. The result is a position paper, policy recommendations, and an action plan for implementation. Additional outcomes are increased coordination and communication among state agency representatives and expanded knowledge among a broad cross section of participants at both the state and community levels.

Current ILRDC Family Literacy Services include:

- Technical Assistance to match providers with program models to suit the needs of their client groups.
- Collaborative efforts to promote productive field work.
- Publishing newsletters on family literacy programs and policies.
- Organization of an annual statewide family literacy conference.
- Workshops and training on family literacy program planning and implementation.

Project Lifelong Learning

Project Lifelong Learning is the result of a grant from the United States Department of Education, Office of Educational Research and Improvement (OERI) to The Institute for the Study for Adult Literacy at Penn State. Working with WPSX-TV (Penn State) and WQED (Pittsburgh, PA), the Institute has produced materials to advance Goal #5 of the National Education Goals. This partnership has developed public service announcements, documentaries, and staff development videos with accompanying print materials which focus on 1) the workplace/workforce, 2) the community, and 3) the family.

Staff at the Institute have identified five successful strategies used in literacy programs around the country and is available from the Penn State Institute for the Study of Adult Literacy. The family literacy print and non-print materials are useful for business, industry, community leaders, and parents. The video presentation examines successful programs in Maine, New York, and Arizona and presents a context for policy makers and program providers to envision how a successful family program might work.

2
COLLABORATION AND FAMILY LITERACY: NATURAL PARTNERS?

The term *collaboration* combined with *family literacy* cuts across both human and child service fields. Collaborations are an outgrowth of a realization that programs can be more effective when they explore ways to reshape the delivery of goods and services. Sharon Kagan of Yale University has written extensively about the history of collaboration for child care and early education services. She comments that although many people are currently engaged in "experiments in collaboration" among agencies serving the overlapping needs of different populations, there is a pronounced lack of systematic investigation about the evolution of collaboration as a social construct. However, observation of some successful collaborative ventures has identified goal setting, the sharing of resources, power, and authority, and the need for some degree of flexibility among participants as necessary components of a successful collaboration.

Key Elements

In the course of developing a statewide project, the authors were struck by the complexity of the interrelationships which were revealed during the 16-month case study on the process of collaboration. The project is described in detail in Appendix A. The chart in Figure 2-1, Key Elements of Collaboration in Support of Family Literacy, conceptualizes the different possible levels of collaboration which exist in Massachusetts. These elements, arrayed in three levels by categories, display the collaborative process and the interrelationships among them. The chart suggests and summarizes the complexity of the collaborations. Not surprisingly, the relationships between partners at other levels had an impact on the success (or failure) of a community collaboration. Because of the new approach presented by family literacy, it is sometimes difficult for the participants to visualize any level other than the one in which they are currently involved. The chart presents the framework for a better understanding of the context of state collaborations.

The elements of the *Key Characteristics of Collaboration* are described below:

Level 1: On-site collaboration (Level 1) involves service/program deliverers and is the most local level of implementation of a family literacy collaboration. It is on-site where direct service to participant families takes place. Although the program itself may operate on a full- or part-time basis, it is through daily or weekly personal contacts between staff/staff and staff/families that support for the program services is developed and maintained. This level must operate by team effort to ensure the smooth functioning of the program. The true essence of collaboration is found in joining the skills of persons from several agencies with differing expertise and melding them into an integrated program. Joint training to work out details among collaborative team members will provide clear delineations of responsibilities. Parents' input is important to the operation of Level 1 collaboration. A mechanism for their input is integral to training and should identify and respond to any obstacles to parent participation and retention which is critical to success at this level.

The challenge at the program level is for all participants to respect each other's knowledge and skills and to accept everyone's individuality. This is not always easy to achieve. The intensity of collaborations at this level revolves around frequent personal interactions, so flexibility and adaptability of staff is important. Even successful programs find themselves bogged down in the details of running demanding programs, and find it necessary to take time out to renew or refresh the human, personal spirit of collaboration which is so central to operations and a healthy working climate. Members of Level 1 interact primarily with individuals at Level 2, in addition to one another.

Level 2. The community collaboration level (Level 2) is intensive because at this level members represent their individual agencies or organizations. Directors or managers work at this level, and the challenge is to maintain the integrity of their own agencies while allowing for the necessary negotiation and adjustment with other agencies. Members must develop shared goals to benefit the participant group. This may entail giving up some individual agencies' power or authority in order to develop a successful project or service. Members must have authority to speak for their agencies in the community planning process. Otherwise the process may get stalled or delayed. Critical for success at this level is the communication between the designated representative and the agency director (if this member is not the director). Agreements for integration of resources, adjusted to local conditions, are settled at this level and may include informal or formal written memorandums of understanding. Most agencies usually want some visibility in a joint project, and it is at this level that communication, including announcements about the collaboration, are generated to the media. This group may meet more frequently or intensively in the early planning stages, but generally will meet less frequently than Level 1 members. They also may meet at different agencies on a rotating basis in order to gain a better understanding about the site, services, and role of each organization within the collaboration.

Level 3. The state or corporate administration level is where most policy and regulations are made. Ordinarily, Level 3 is the visionary collaboration or the "big picture" level, although the "big picture" sometimes emerges from Level 1 and Level 2 interactions as well and should also be fostered and supported there. The state directors of Adult Basic Education, State Library Agency, Chapter One, Even Start, Head Start, and other organizations must respond to external mandates and coordinate their own activities. Visionary leadership at this level is essential to connect those with influence to authorize far-reaching changes across agencies through collaboration. For example, Level 3 can contribute several important things. Policy directors can provide incentives for collaboration through issuing Requests for Proposals (RFP) or contracts for service which require collaboration as a basis for funding. They can also provide and identify relevant technical assistance, joint evaluation, and dedicated moneys like federal set asides.

For example, these agencies might respond to the mandate of the National Literacy Act to set up an advisory council on adult education that includes a representative cross section of agencies involved in literacy.

There are several political issues which sometimes get in the way of participation in support of collaboration. Matters of turf protection and mandates may interfere. Therefore, the blessing of Level 3 participants is extremely helpful, some say essential, to set new priorities for collaboration at Levels 2 and 1. Members at Level 3 may be housed within the same organizations (i.e., State Department of Education) but historically, may seldom interact, initiate, or maintain collaboration in the absence of directives to do so. Also, many state agencies must interact with Federal agencies which may mandate or otherwise direct state agencies to respond in a manner which discourages collaboration. Hopefully, this too will change during the decade of the 90s.

Lessons Learned

THE MASSACHUSETTS COMMUNITY COLLABORATIONS FOR FAMILY LITERACY MODEL

When the Massachusetts Community Collaboration for Family Literacy model was conceived (see Appendix A), there were few pre-established ideas about what would be the ultimate project outcome. The early experiment in collaboration experienced by the authors left a lingering impression about its importance as

FIGURE 2.1. Key Elements of Collaboration in Support of Family Literacy

KEY ELEMENTS OF COLLABORATION IN SUPPORT OF FAMILY LITERACY

LEVEL	MEMBERS	CHARACTERISTICS	STRUCTURE	RESOURCES COMMITTED	FACILITATIVE ACTIVITIES
LEVEL 3 *State and/or Corporate*	State Directors of: Adult Education; Chapter I; Head Start; Even Start; State Librarian; Corporate Director of Public Relations; Other appropriate designees	Systems orientation; Mandates or encourages local collaborations; Initiates/implements state policies; State and Federal political considerations; Networks with multiple agencies; Formal written agreements; Formal leadership; Quarterly meetings (or less frequently); Mandated or voluntary origin	Agencies maintain separate identities and missions; Targets overlapping client groups; Delegates representative as decision maker; Requires written agreement; Maintains line relationships with Level 2	Supports technical assistance consultant; Dedicates state monies and federal set asides; Provides incentives for participation; Sponsors shared training events; Provides resources and collections on family literacy	Initiates interagency collaborative policy agenda; Issues joint plans for RFP format, process; Initiates joint program evaluation; Arranges joint funding and funding cycle; Conducts Informational and Bidders' Conference; Disseminates information; Arranges for training; Communicates with Level 2
LEVEL 2 *Local Community*	Local Directors of: Adult Basic/ESL Education; Chapter I; Head Start; Local Library; Community Agencies; Other appropriate designees	Service area orientation; Initiates or responds to mandate to collaborate; Initiates/implements local community policies; State and local political considerations; Networks with local agencies; Formal written agreements; Collegial leadership Monthly meetings (or more frequently); Mandated or voluntary origin	Gain of new group identity and focus on shared mission; Targets overlapping client groups; Individual decision-makers from various agencies; Requires written agreements; Maintains line relationships with Levels 1 and 3	Supports representative to collaborative; Dedicates a portion of funds and resources; Responds to incentives for participation; Publicizes activities of collaboration and focus on family literacy; Arranges for joint training; Supports joint referrals; Distributes resource materials	Develops, administers, maintains collaboration; Develops shared mission for joint planning; Conducts joint training; needs assessment; Writes funding proposal; Disseminates information; Develops job criteria for staff; Communicates with Levels 1 and 3
LEVEL 1 *Program Site*	Teachers of: Adult Basic/ESL Education; Chapter I; Head Start; Adult Services/Children's Librarians; Volunteer Tutors; Home Visitors; Parents and children	Participant families orientation; Implements new or combined program; Implements, revises, suggests site policies; Local and site political considerations; Implements collaborative instructional practices; Formal or informal agreements; Team-based case management Weekly or day-to-day contact	Identification as team members with shared mission; Serves diverse client group; Team based decision making; Informal agreements within written framework; Maintains line relationships with Level 2	Supports team-based staff; Provides program space; Provides incentives to client families; Publicizes activities; Attends joint training; Uses joint referrals	Conducts team-based case management program; Implements shared mission; Conducts joint training; curriculum design; joint instruction; Implements center and home-based program special events; Involves parent participation; Communicates infrequently with other Levels

a strategy and the complexities of involving agencies and people at different levels within the community. According to Kagan (1992) the two most important goals of a successful collaboration are the *production of direct services* and the *creation of changes* in an existing system. By these indicators, the Massachusetts model was highly successful.

RESULTS OF THE CCFL PROJECT EXPERIENCE

The following results of the collaborative experience in six communities to develop a plan for family literacy will introduce the reader to the complexities of family literacy service delivery, speak to the nature of collaboration, identify challenges to be faced and barriers to overcome, and suggest possible solutions which might work for others. While much of the following are observations, the experience may be helpful to others planning to embark on similar ventures in their communities. The model of the *Key Elements of Collaboration in Support of Family Literacy* is used to focus on these ideas. The CCFL project was designed to reach participants at Level 2 so they could plan Level 1 programs. The project itself was initiated at Level 3, the State level.

Common to all six projects were the following reasons which were given for participation:

1. There was an incentive to collaborate, e.g. the prospect of future funding and the understanding that agencies would receive some new resources in the form of print and nonprint materials. (Level 3 incentive)
2. Community agencies were hard pressed to meet the needs of parents and children and they acknowledged the need to look at shared resources. (Level 2 need)
3. In most cases, the CCFL project director was able to make contact with more than one agency or organization in each community and present the case for joining a collaboration both verbally and in writing. (Level 2 activity)
4. Some of the adult basic education professionals indicated their willingness to participate in a project coordinated by the state library agency because of their previous positive experience with the Massachusetts Board of Library Commissioners staff around shared issues of adult literacy. (Interaction of Levels 1, 2, and 3)
5. The topic of family literacy was gaining a lot of national attention and, for many human service providers, the concept of addressing the needs of the family as a whole made good sense and they were willing to learn more about it. (Level 2 interest)
6. Some groups had prior experience with community collaborations, although not at quite the same level of activity. However, their experience had been positive and they were willing to consider working together. (Level 2 experience)

7. For some, there was the perception that being involved in what was designated as an innovative or discrete "special project" would be worthwhile and they would be getting some technical assistance along the way. (Level 2 incentive)

The CCFL experience, joining in new community collaborations for the purpose of planning for community needs in family literacy (Level 1 projects), has been a learning experience for the project team and participants alike. While some experiences were particular to this project, many will be reflected in projects which others may develop.

Conducting Successful Collaborations

The elements of a successful Level 2 collaboration include the following:

- Involving the key players.
- Assessing the contributions that each participant could contribute to the project.
- Achieving a shared vision for a family literacy project.
- Developing a project design that all members can support.
- Fostering a climate that allows for diverging opinions and ideas setting attainable, achievable objectives for the shared project.
- Assigning tasks for carrying out project design.
- Building a feeling of ownership at both interagency and intra-agency levels.
- Providing a mechanism to deal with misunderstandings or barriers.
- Beginning to institutionalize change within organizations which would ultimately affect the delivery or development of improved services.
- Communicating the success of a collaborative effort.

CHARACTERISTIC OUTCOMES

Among the factors experienced by the most successful Level 2 collaborations were:

1. They included representatives from at least three different community agencies: i.e. libraries, adult literacy providers, Chapter One (a school program for "at risk" children), or daycare/Head Start programs.
2. Teams met more frequently than the four meetings suggested (during a nine month planning period).
3. Teams had an agenda with short-term objectives to accomplish at each meeting. They respected each others' busy schedules and dismissed the meeting when the work for each was accomplished. Because of this approach, small-step projects emerged such as the jointly sponsored book-

mobile in one community. It helped to build a trust relationship and immediately proved the value of collaboration.

4. Someone from a participating agency assumed a leadership role, either self-selected or delegated, with the group's approval.

5. The community began by identifying and articulating the role each group already provided in support of literacy within the family. Without this step, there was a lack of understanding about missions, goals, and constraints. Even in small communities, many people had not met before they began participating in this project. For example, the community mapping exercise enabled the group to plot the location of agencies and facilities for each town, discussing transportation, opening hours, and jointly exploring the advantages and disadvantages of each locale.

6. Individuals met and talked with participants from other communities with the same jobs and philosophies, as well as with different agencies in their communities. This expanded general and specific knowledge of differing and similar perspectives. This also verified the missions of agencies which were previously unknown.

7. Teams all attended the large group meetings where they developed a common understanding of the goals of the project and also defined the components of family literacy programs. They were able to share experiences which reduced isolation and built camaraderie. Traveling together in one car to meetings also strengthened a burgeoning network and helped people become acquainted better.

8. Teams were composed for the most part by persons with the authority to make decisions for the agency. In those agencies that were not so represented, the shadow of absent decision makers reduced the credibility of the representative to others and slowed down the development of trust relationships.

9. Level 2 members disseminated information about family literacy across agencies and within their own organizations; spreading the family literacy/collaboration concept to a larger group of people and helping to establish ownership and support.

10. Teams and individuals began to adapt a broader vision of service delivery in a community-wide and family oriented sense, rather than focusing on a narrow vision of community and services to individuals.

11. Collaborations began to envision themselves playing new roles in community partnerships with other social and educational agencies. The value of partnerships and coordinated services became more "real" through this project and unified their visions. The word community became less of a concept and more of an operating strategy.

12. Teams began to institutionalize their mission as serving families rather than individuals—for example, one group began to incorporate family literacy into their long-range planning goals.

13. They learned that all "models of practice" (Level 1 projects) need to be tailored to location conditions, and that as a team, they had the judgment necessary to do this planning.

14. They learned that the richer the mixture of team participation, the more resources were available for the community.
15. They accepted that there were a variety of ways of conducting family literacy programs.
16. Finally, they discovered that "collaboration" is a process that can be learned—skills like conflict management, understanding the values and motivations of others, and dealing with difficult personalities can be learned through training—and that more training in this process would be helpful.

In order to determine whether stated project outcomes were met, a series of questions were used to frame a response from CCFL participants.

Interview Responses

An increasing amount of literature on collaborative efforts is being written. In two monographs published by the Education and Human Services Consortium, *What it Takes: Structuring Interagency Partnerships to Connect Children and Families with Comprehensive Services* and *Thinking Collaboratively: Ten Questions and Answers to Help Policy Makers Improve Services to Children,* certain guidelines for the development of cooperative collaborations and partnerships have been identified. The following questions adapted from these two sources were used to provide a context for interviews with community participants at the end of the project year about their role in moving a collaborative project forward.

1. Did These Groups Involve All the Key Players?

In the communities that participated in this project the following community agencies were among those represented as partners in local collaborations:

- Public library
- Head Start
- Department of Public Welfare
- Local school: Chapter One directors, school librarians, teachers, administrators, special education, bilingual education
- Regional vocational/technical high school
- Community college/state college
- Adult learning center
- United Way
- Neighborhood Community Center
- Chamber of Commerce
- Community Action Center
- Private Industry Council
- Literacy Volunteers
- Daycare providers

- Even Start
- Employment and training center
- Girl scouts
- Local foundations
- Service clubs (e.g. Rotary)
- Criminal justice department-juvenile offenders
- Local prison/jail
- Family shelter
- Cable television company.

In those projects which were most successful, representatives from the library, adult literacy, children's services, and Chapter One programs were all active participants. This meant that each agency representative could speak on the issue of developing and providing services from the point of view of the child or the adult or in some cases, of both. In those cases which were most successful the group met more often than was suggested by the CCFL proposal. One community which had already developed a family program met weekly, while another group met at least eight times from December until September. This group was represented by the director of the library, the director of Chapter One, and the director of Adult Basic Education, demonstrating a high level of commitment to the process.

In one collaboration, three separate municipalities were involved in developing a project which would take place at multiple locations. However daunting a task, one adult basic educator noted that these communities have had a long history of successful cooperation. Again, this group included the participation of program directors who were at the top of their organizations. Their executive positions enabled them to make decisions critical to the direction of the program. Early in the process, the group received support from a local Opportunity Council, which is a community based employment and training agency. Of the six collaboratives, this group achieved the broadest support among diverse agencies which included representatives from business, employment and training, welfare, the criminal justice system, and a local children's service center.

Moreover, this collaborative formed at a time when the local United Way hired a new director. The group was in an opportune position to provide input into United Way's literacy needs assessment for the region. This placed the group in a strong position to not only identify service gaps but to focus on future needs and ultimately to have an impact on an overall economic plan for their region.

The library director observed that had she not been her organization's principal representative, it might have been more difficult. As the director of the library she succeeded in getting a correspondingly high level of attention from the group. She stated had she not been the representative, it would have been extremely important for her to attend the initial meeting in order to show support for the person designated as the liaison with the group.

2. Were your teams able to come up with a realistic strategy that all members could support?

A critical factor in the success of this project was the ability for each community to identify the strengths or knowledge which they brought to their individual group. Of the six communities participating in this project, three developed a collaborative plan that actively involved the library as a site for adult or family literacy. One developed a strategy in which the library would serve as a resource center for families receiving adult literacy instruction at another location and one focused on developing a relationship between Chapter One families and the library. The final community will continue to implement its existing family program involving the library although the site has been changed. In almost all cases, those communities which were most successful began by identifying and articulating the role which their agency played in support of literacy within the family. This was a critical first step because in a number of cases, there was a lack of understanding among groups about mission, purpose, and resources.

In one community, a first and extremely positive step was to develop a citywide Family Literacy Directory for purposes of program information and referral, hours, and resources in service to families. In another community, the group conducted a very thorough community needs assessment, complete with graphs and charts, which gave the group an excellent idea of the service population and where gaps needed to be filled. It also advanced this group's proposal writing ability. The same data was available for different agencies to use when applying for funding from different sources in support of a shared plan for family literacy.

It was especially important to conduct a needs assessment which would look at the data in a new way, e.g. how can different sources of data be brought together to make a case for family literacy. Those communities which were involved in a thorough needs assessment were better able to define their role within the collaborative. As a result, it was easier for the group to develop a sound proposal—one which all members could support.

In some communities, the issue of turf had to be raised in order to clear the air. Some adults may have been receiving adult literacy services and these same adults needed to be targeted by Chapter One directors for parental involvement. Within the context of this project, the library was frequently perceived as a neutral agency which would be able to apply for funds from a discrete funding source on behalf of a plan which would benefit the community as a whole. Moreover, it was understood that only the library was eligible for these LSCA funds. For many groups, the more they worked together the greater their comfort level became in addressing shared issues.

By identifying the mission and purpose of each agency vis-a-vis a family program, different agencies began to see how they could approach a variety of sources to fund a family program which would coordinate services from various agencies and ultimately benefit from a shared client group.

In order to build a shared vision, community participants needed to carefully articulate the goals that their collective organizations could support. In one community, that vision was in place after five months of intensive planning. The Chapter One Director became so convinced of the viability of the family approach that she put a tremendous amount of energy into writing an Even Start grant. They were one of two communities successful in obtaining that grant in the state. In subsequent discussions, team members acknowledged the value of the CCFL planning meetings in the achievement of this highly competitive award.

Because the state library agency had suggested that a well designed plan would result in funding, most communities were willing to become involved in this process. One library director cautioned that you cannot call a group together just to plan as "an exercise." She stated, "You need to organize with a focus." The possibility of funding provides that focus.

In almost all cases, the role of the library in this project was to serve as a resource for families to come together. In four communities, the library has decided to designate one room as a family learning center. These resource rooms will be stocked with craft tables, comfortable chairs, a rug, and some bookshelves. They will contain many of the preliteracy materials which low literate families do not have in their homes. In some cases, the target families for the family program will include adults who are already receiving literacy instruction at another site. In other instances, the library will contract with an adult education agency to provide on-site instruction for adults including computer-assisted learning for both parents and children.

3. Did your teams develop a communication process which allowed for divergent opinions and ideas?

In those groups which kept closest to a schedule, one person generally assumed responsibility for setting the agenda, but all members of the group participated. Those groups which kept to their agenda and met the short term objectives—e.g. bringing data for a needs assessment or initiating contacts with a children's service agency—seemed to be most successful in developing a completed plan. One group had such an outstanding record of staying on schedule that they were close to writing a finished proposal even before the letter of intent stage. The challenge in any collaborative effort is that the group must begin to click or develop a synergy, or they may end up spending a lot of time and resources spinning their wheels.

4. Did your teams set attainable, achievable objectives for the shared project?

In most cases, the individual communities have yet to test their plans, yet in a number of cases, the act of working together allowed the completion of some short term objectives which moved the organizations closer towards the goal of a shared project (Level 1). For example, in one community as a result of the cooperative effort, the children's librarian went to the Even Start center and met with parents, and Even Start staff brought parents and children to the library to sign up for library cards. Additionally, the children's librarian was invited by the Chapter One director to participate in a workshop to make Big Books and flannel boards.

The summer after the initial collaboration began, an Even Start staff member joined the children's librarian on the bookmobile for a weekly visit to housing projects and day care centers in the community. They secured a source for book giveaways, shared storytelling, and involved families in crafts at these centers. This was a highly successful, achievable activity which grew out of a collaborative relationship between the agencies. It also served as a possible objective for a future shared project.

5. Did your teams keep your goal of a working, family literacy project as a planning objective?

The majority of those interviewed cited the value of the December training session which presented different models of family literacy and discussed the importance of community mapping and basic needs assessment instruction as vital to the subsequent positive outcome of successful planning meetings. This training provided a common understanding of what different model programs might look like and enabled communities to envision the components of a successful program in their individual communities.

It is clearly important to provide training for communities on how to set up a collaboration. The visits made by the project director and educational consultant provided a link to all other projects and gave those interested in planning an opportunity to ask questions which were viewed as helpful by the groups. Throughout the project year local collaboration teams had an opportunity to interact with one another both at the June conference and again in September. In the evaluation session most participants expressed interest in maintaining an "ongoing support group" for a statewide family literacy. Community collaborators and others who attended the first conference continue to discuss the possibility of planning and holding a second statewide family literacy conference.

In one community, after numerous months of trying to make the collaboration work with two communities, the library decided to focus on a project which would begin with "smaller steps" by working in cooperation with Chapter One.

6. Were your teams able to build ownership within the collaborative at both intra-agency and interagency levels?

From the experience of this project, collaboration must work at several levels. It is critical to build a sense of trust among different providers before focusing on developing a collaborative project.

When the agency or library director was the principal collaborator, that person had the ability to make decisions which would be backed up by the group. It was the general consensus of those interviewed that if the library director is not the primary participant he or she must back up the person through a visible presence at the first meeting. It is important to show that its representative has the authority to speak for the institution, an important Level 2 function.

In at least two communities, the director of the library was more a shadow figure in the whole process. Participants in the group felt that the final plan would have been strengthened by a more active presence from the director.

In another community, a number of parallel initiatives around family literacy had begun to emerge. As a result of the CCFL project, the library was brought more fully into the partnership and the "ad hoc committee for family literacy" became more of a solid, coordinating committee for family literacy within the community. It included participation from 1) adult education; 2) Chapter One; 3) the public library; 4) Headstart; and 5) homeless and family shelters. As the coordinator for Even Start noted, the collaboration kept the various players talking, working, and learning.

One director commented, "You have to sell this project to different layers of people involved in a project." This seems especially true when an agency is involved in a totally new undertaking. Staff at all levels need some basic idea of the project in order to field questions which will inevitably arise when the agency representative is not available.

7. How did your teams work around issues of misunderstandings or barriers to collaborations?

Specific among the barriers/issues confronted by CCFL participants were the following:

- Lack of sufficient authority among some members of group to commit their agency to the final project development.
- Lack of support for an individual who represents the agency.
- Fluctuation in group member composition created an inability to focus on a shared plan.
- Lack of full representation of all the key players, e.g. no adult education program.
- Time constraints on individuals who were attempting to develop a collaboration while still performing their other "real" jobs.
- Turf issues relating to funding and misperception of the CCFL mission by one agency.
- Lack of resources, e.g. money to photocopy material for distribution to all participants.
- State and town economy playing havoc with otherwise well intentioned collaboration, e.g. inability to address issues because of fighting for survival.
- Lack of technical assistance, especially true when specific problems arose in a given community.

In one community, a major barrier was the absence of the full complement of agencies at Level 2. Giving reality to the theory of actively involving support from the library, adult education, Chapter One, as well as family support services would appear to be critical to the design of a successful family project. In one community already on shaky ground, a switch in Chapter One Directors at the beginning of the school year further eroded the group's ability to focus on a final plan. On the other hand, in another community this did not prove to be the case. When the Chapter One Director left her position at the end of the summer, there had been so much credibility built up in the "team approach," it did not seriously impede the project from moving forward.

In one community which was less successful with its collaboration, interested community representatives were unsuccessful in involving the local library. At the outset, the local library director expressed concern about the library "serving as a focus for solving a social problem of such dimensions that our school systems, all with significantly more funds available locally than any public library, have not been able to meet head-on with success." This response came from a potential participant who received the same information as everyone else in the convening letter when invited to join the project. This perception of the library's role within the community as a passive place for literacy activities to occur is not uncommon, nor is disgruntlement over the much higher school budgets.

Another factor not to be overlooked in this community was that the adult literacy component was represented by a dedicated professor at a local state college who taught Adult Basic Education. However, there was no existing adult education program. As a result of the above barriers, the first community joined forces with an adjacent municipality in an attempt to involve component groups from both communities to make up a "working team." Again, the second community's working adult education program chose not to participate. Over the months, the composition of the group fluctuated from meeting to meeting with new players showing up at each scheduled meeting where the whole purpose of the project had to be explained again. In the end, the core members from both towns were unable to focus on a plan which would equally meet the needs of all partners in the collaborative. As recently as the final interviews, some participants were expressing concerns about how to recruit potential adult learners to a family program. When the deadline for the final proposal drew near, the library director of one community was unable to convince the local fiscal authority to subcontract grant funds to another community. As a result this group decided to divide and to seek separate funding sources. Since this was the only attempt at collaboration which lacked an active adult education program as a partner, one might infer that this may have been a contributing factor to the problems of the project design.

One difficulty experienced by most communities was how to best involve local Head Start and daycare centers. One director commented that the school-public library relationship was fairly good before this project began, but it was harder to involve local Head Start. For example, in one community the Head Start program is located in an Industrial Park outside of the main community area. Therefore, lack of transportation for children or children and parents to get to the library continues to be a barrier and the group needs to investigate a source of funding to address this issue.

In some communities, it was a slow process to learn how to work together and to put aside individual, short-term goals in favor of a longer look at the impact which a collaborative project would have on the community. Those groups which had the most success were able to demonstrate that the collaborative group was in itself one of the best selling points to funders. Indeed, the LSCA Title VI grant round deadline was delayed for five weeks in order to respond to the goals of *America 2000*. Prospective proposal writers were informed that they could receive an added 15 points to their proposal by showing how well they were collaborating and cooperating with other providers.

8. How did the project begin to institutionalize changes?

Among the most significant changes which took place within a 16-month period were:

- The concept of family literacy began to be considered within the overall planning goals of both libraries and adult educators.
- Adult literacy professionals began to speak more about adult *and* family literacy rather than literacy by itself.
- Community members became aware of the collaborative and began to ask questions which indicated a growing understanding of the concept of family literacy.

In one library, the short-term goals of designing a family literacy project ended up being incorporated into the library's overall planning goals. Currently, the MBLC is requiring long-range planning as a requirement for future LSCA funding. Therefore, many libraries are actively going through a formal planning process. The children's librarian noted that family literacy activities were identified as an important role and as a result have been written into the library's overall plan of service.

In another community, the director of adult basic education, who teaches by day in the school system, began to coordinate visits of middle school students to the public library on a weekly basis. The public library director remarked that this activity was a direct result of the adult education director's increasing involvement in the community collaboration. His positive relationship with the library staff prompted a better understanding of how to utilize the library in another aspect of his work—one which would ultimately have a positive benefit on the literacy level of middle school students.

Publicizing the work of the collaboration through newspaper articles and announcements at agency staff meetings seemed to raise awareness that the group was working together. One director commented that after a year of collaboration the local school superintendent queries, "What's going on and what are you going to do next?" Publicity about the project seems to have a positive effect and create community interest and involvement.

As a result of this project, three community libraries will institutionalize a new service, such as a library family learning center as described above. This is a new approach to serving families which will be linked with other community agencies serving a shared target group.

INTERVIEW SUMMARY

Collaborative relationships at all levels are the means to reach ends, not ends in themselves. The fact that a group continues to meet but does not move forward to accomplish its stated goals may be an indication that the group is unable to focus. Collaborative relationships may begin to identify the points where multiple providers serve the same target audience. Alone, however, they are often not able to proceed because of external factors such as inadequate funding or lack of transportation to programs. Those who collaborate as representatives of their organization must be fully supported by their administration and given the necessary time to spend on articulating the relationships among all partners. Collaborative efforts are time consuming. In many cases, participants will need further training in problem solving, how to conduct effective meetings, and how to resolve conflicts in order to avoid problems related to turf issues.

Participating agencies should ask themselves before embarking on this process how effective they are in reaching and serving clients if they continue on their present course and how the development of a collaborative relationship might improve services to this shared, overlapping client group?

Observations On Building Collaborations

Overall, the CCFL project encouraged collaboration and cooperation around planning for family literacy in local communities where previously, none had existed. Revealing observations were made as CCFL participants spoke of their common objectives for recruiting and serving hard-to-reach clients, which, in many instances, resulted in recruiting the *same* target families for services by individual agencies or organizations. (We wondered, if in better times, this realization went unacknowledged or just unspoken.) Reduction in redundancy is one potential cost saving result of increased community collaborations.

Staff members spoke of reaching out to meet others in the participating communities who, without the opportunities provided by the CCFL experience, would not have met in the course of their professional responsibilities. Under normal conditions, Chapter One administrators, housed in school or administrative buildings of the local education authority, would have little opportunity or need to meet officially with local librarians. Similarly, adult basic education administrators and teachers, while perhaps aware of the local libraries' resources, may not have physically entered these settings, nor made themselves aware of the actual and potential services offered by the libraries. In-school professionals (Chapter One) rarely, if ever, met out-of-school colleagues such as ABE or Head Start members. Thus, the project drew together a variety of service providers with similar organizational missions who previously had little or no knowledge of each others' organizational missions and resources.

It would seem that economic hardships fostered collaborations in local communities. Collaborations may coalesce more easily as a result of shared economic woes. For better or worse, when resources are readily available, the motivation to share them is reduced and individual organizations' turf is better protected. Making do with less coupled with the realization that nearly all workers and organizations are vulnerable seems to increase the desire to collaborate among the CCFL participants.

As a result of cutbacks, travel reimbursements were harder to obtain, which affected staff participation in CCFL events. Emergency meetings forced participants to choose among priorities, in which organizational needs were understandably primary among the participants. These are but a few of the indicators of the hostile conditions in the local communities we asked to join the project and a few examples of impacts on the project itself.

The Statewide invitational conference, *Building Community Collaborations for Family Literacy,* was a vital activity in the project according to follow-up evaluations of the conference. This event provided a rich, one-day immersion experience in the concepts and practices of family literacy. It contributed to knowledge through its seminars and workshops, it informed and motivated action, and was itself an example of multidisciplinary collaboration; gathering the resources of Adult Basic, Early Childhood, Head-Start, and Chapter One educators and administrators, representatives from state and local education associations, and staff from a wide variety of organizations. It facilitated networking and acknowledged those working in the CCFL project. It cemented the concept of family literacy as a priority effort and emphasized the benefits of its collaborative approach.

Incentives were important for participation in the project. In an ideal world, good will alone might motivate human service workers to plan together in a spirit of cooperation. This benevolent attitude, however, is not encouraged in many organizations. Indeed, the most evident models for the provision of services at the federal and state level have promoted separate and parallel activities. Cross agency planning has been neglected, and in many ways, discouraged. Now, the benefits of collaborations are beginning to emerge. Better integration of services and holistic planning for disadvantaged populations is an important agenda for the last decade of the twentieth century.

In the CCFL project, barriers to collaboration were anticipated at the outset. The major incentive, in the form of possible seed money for a collaborative community project, was a special motivating factor. In times of economic stress, new sources of resources are essential to operating human service programs. Enlightened self interest propelled the community teams into an experience, however reluctantly initiated, which becomes an exciting new way to interact on behalf of at-risk families.

As a result of greater interest in family literacy, the Massachusetts Department of Education, Bureau of Adult Education, created a position within its department to work as a liaison around family literacy issues. Within the past year, the adult education support network, SABES, identified family literacy as an important priority for adult education professionals at two of the five regional sites. The bureau also earmarked money to go for program training. Because of the availability of new funds, several library-based literacy programs were successful in applying for and receiving training moneys earmarked for family literacy.

3
STEPS TO CONSIDER WHEN DEVELOPING A COLLABORATIVE PROJECT

Implications

The implications for practice which emerged from observing the development of six collaborations may be helpful to communities seeking to develop their own programs. They can be divided into three areas:

- Designing or initiating a collaboration.
- Implementing a collaboration.
- Sustaining the work of the collaboration over time.

THE DESIGN/INITIATION PHASE

Successful collaborations take place over time. The key to the success is building trust among participants. Many collaborations which begin as informal meetings frequently move towards more formal arrangements as a shared vision or project begins to take place. This may take a period of years and participants must learn that, in the beginning, good will may not be enough to encourage a process which frequently does not facilitate speed.

The issue of turf continues to be a formidable barrier to successful collaboration. Sometimes a reluctance to participate in initial meetings may be a subtle sign that one member is protecting the agency's territorial mission.

Team participation in activities such as working on a force field analysis, identifying key players, and working together on a community mapping exercise are among the training activities critical to a successful collaboration (see Figures 4.2., 4.3., and 4.4.).

ELEMENTS FOR EFFECTIVE TECHNICAL ASSISTANCE

The collaboration group may need additional technical assistance in the following areas:

- How-to conduct a needs assessment of the community which identifies the values of the target group.
- How-to understand the values of the different groups in the collaboration.
- How a group learns to agree on some common values.
- How-to listen respectfully to others' opinions.
- How-to set priorities for project objectives, e.g. starting with the most easily achievable objectives.
- How-to determine what resources are *available* compared with resources that are *needed* to serve the project.
- How-to identify the autonomy of individual players in the partnership and how to help them communicate their agency's position within the group.
- How-to ensure communication between the parent organization to the partnership and how to "report back."
- How-to identify the process for conflict resolution to reach consensus.

IMPLEMENTATION

As collaboration moves from the design to the implementation phase, it is important to note that the skills of conflict resolution need to be operational. A series of written guidelines and policies, which are mutually agreed upon early, may help to head off potential problems. Participants must avoid getting sidetracked from the purpose of collaboration as differences in agency mission, operating budgets, or even pay scale emerge as part of the process.

The selection of agencies to participate in the *core team* is frequently related to a desire to maintain an *optimal* size. A group which is perceived as too exclusive is as likely to suffer as a group which keeps growing because it is trying to include everybody.

SUSTAINING AND FOCUSING THE COLLABORATION

As people continue to meet together, a new comfort level frequently emerges. On the other hand, the issue of governance or who controls the collaborative may be raised. A high turnover among members should be avoided and may weaken the group. Because members of a family literacy collaborative will be primarily representatives of human services agencies, it is a given that these agencies will be subjected to fluctuations in budget, staff, and cut-backs in services. This may well have an effect on the ability of individuals to focus.

While collaborative groups may share many common characteristics, each community is unique in the makeup of its agencies and organizations along with the individuals whom they represent. A community collaboration has the potential to be highly successful at improving services within a complex system if it can be harnessed around a single mission—the improvement of services to families.

Guidelines

The following guidelines emerged from the experience of working with Level 2 collaborations:

1. Community groups should agree on a local need, or at least agree to work with other community providers to fully determine that need.
2. The library or agency taking the lead needs to identify other core members of the community group and to seek to involve them in the cooperative development of a community-wide plan for family literacy.
3. The group should identify a meeting space. It is often helpful to rotate meetings to different community sites in order to familiarize participants with the resources of each partner.
4. Teams may require learning some new skills and may need to participate in a training exercise in community mapping and how to conduct effective meetings.
5. Participants should share as much information as possible within their group. The provision of photocopies of monographs, articles, or a resource collection on family literacy is useful towards developing a shared knowledge and a shared vision. If a local business or private sector partner is part of the collaborative, perhaps they can contribute photocopying, postage, or a small amount of money to pay for this. Photocopying an important, low-cost, and necessary support service which should be provided.
6. Groups should hold their meetings at established meeting times and try to accomplish small, concrete, achievable objectives at each meeting.
7. Groups which have trouble focusing may need to bring in some-one with experience as a facilitator to help the group get back on track.

ELEVEN STEPS FOR STATE POLICY MAKERS

Policy makers at Level 3 should consider the following steps when addressing the need to develop policy at the state level:

1. Make Family Literacy a Priority.
    It is helpful to local programs if there is state policy which sets a priority for the development of family literacy programs. Without a doubt, most

federal and state authorities place a heavy emphasis on the willingness to cooperate with other providers without attending to their abilities to do so or confirming the intent with concrete memoranda.

2. Statewide technical assistance.

The training workshops given to the core group of participants was critical to the success of the projects. People need to have a shared knowledge base—a firm understanding of the definitions of family literacy and the elements of a successful program. It is helpful if they can read about, or even better, see a model program. They should be able to receive assistance from other program providers who have experience in running a family literacy program.

3. Provide resources.

The incentive for funding and location of possible resources is also important. Although the final amount, in many cases, which the library might have been able to apply for was small, in comparison to the funds given by Even Start, it nonetheless served as a catalyst to begin working together. The participants always had the goal in front of them: a deadline for developing a response to the RFP.

It is important to provide resources for participants as they develop a plan. Such topics as emergent literacy, early schooling, parenting, and titles on family literacy program models (such as *Parents as Reading Partners* or *Family Reading*) will be helpful in developing and supporting the concept of family literacy. A small grant could be provided which would enable programs to buy an initial collection of board books, concept books, or alphabet books which would form the beginning of a family learning center.

4. Provide technical expertise in family literacy.

Because of the emerging nature of family literacy and that a variety of programs are based within different areas (e.g. adult basic education, libraries, early childhood) it is imperative that policy decisions reflect knowledge and expertise of this complicated new field. This work should be coordinated by one agency which has the knowledge and understanding of the diverse delivery system and target groups involved. That agency should be in regular communication with other state and local providers in order to widely disseminate information about the importance of family literacy programs.

At present a number of agencies are seeking to address a piece of the family literacy agenda. Chapter One, Head Start, Adult Education, and other programs may need to examine their guidelines for funding programs which could provide support for family literacy. In Massachusetts, state agencies have been discussing the development of a common RFP for service.

5. Provide training.

State-level agancies need to provide technical assistance as well as training in program design. Given the finite amount of resources available and the nature of family literacy, improved coordination and collaboration at both state and local levels is needed among those serving families.

6. Encourage partnerships with the private sector.

   It is significant that the private sector has taken an interest in family literacy. Local businesses and private foundations such as Bell Atlantic should be encouraged to enter into partnerships in support of family programs. Moreover, as a way of generating more support, it would be important to showcase successful efforts as a way of attracting more private sector support.

7. Extend workplace programs.

   Those programs which already offer a workplace education program should be encouraged to consider adding a family component as a way of successfully enhancing an existing program.

8. Target women and children.

   Specific efforts must continue to address the needs of women in poverty including minorities, teenage mothers, and single heads of households. Research has shown that investment in the education of women yields multiple positive results. As the need for more highly educated workers grows, the labor force will need more women with higher level skills who, as parents, are the most important factor in the success of their children regardless of gender.

9. Reduce barriers to collaboration.

   In order for family programs to be effective, it is imperative to remove the barriers experienced by almost every human service program—a terrible cycle of frantic proposal writing aimed at ensuring funding year after year. Evidence to date suggests that family literacy programs seem to work and programs that receive stable, long-term funding become established and flourish.

10. Evaluate programs appropriately.

    These programs need to fine tune their program design through ongoing evaluation which will meaningfully measure the impact of the program upon both adults and children.

11. Support participative multicultural planning.

    Given the changing demographics, family literacy programs should fully acknowledge and reflect the specific needs of a growing number of bicultural or multicultural participants while continuing to involve these parents in the planning and design of their own programs.

THREE STEPS FOR THE STATE LIBRARY AGENCY STAFF

1. Provide incentives.

   The state library agency must provide leadership to begin local community collaborations for those that are not field-initiated. It is therefore necessary to provide collaboration incentives in the form of potential funding and technical assistance in order to get the collaboration going or to further encourage cooperation where an initial structure exists.

2. Link state policy makers.

If the state library agency staff is known to have experience with family literacy programs, they will possess more credibility when initiating these projects at the local level. The establishment of a policy level collaboration (level four) suggests that there will be greater chance for success at other levels. If the state director of adult basic education, state coordinator of Chapter One and Head Start as well as the State Librarian (or similar state-level coordinator) can view this as a jointly developed project, other interested policy makers may be brought into the discussion. The linkage of state policy makers is fundamental in order to reinforce the need for a shared vision of cooperative planning for family literacy at all levels.

3. Create resource centers.

A resource collection is fundamental to the development of family programs. A state library, state level adult education provider, or Chapter One should maintain a basic collection of family literacy materials and at minimum an extensive resource list of materials which would be useful for beginning a family literacy collection. Access to these materials early was a factor in the successful planning and implementation of a family literacy project. When materials were purchased for community collaboration members they could be shared with others and provided a wealth of ideas about what a program might look like. The increasing number of video programs available are especially useful when presenting the concept of family literacy to both parents and caregivers. The resource collection in Appendix E lists some of the material which was found most useful.

SECTION TWO

4
THE COMMUNITY COLLABORATION PROCESS

Step One: Inviting Participants to the Collaboration

The material in the following guidelines was developed with the technical assistance of Cristine Smith, a literacy training specialist at World Education in Boston. This information was used to train people in the six Massachusetts collaborative projects. The participants found this process useful in advancing their local collaborations.

The origins of a collaborative effort may be mandated by an outside funding source or it may be the spontaneous convergence of community providers looking for new solutions to unsolved problems. The first meeting may come about because one individual convenes a group at the community level to explore the issues of literacy and its impact on parents and children. On the other hand, the increasing call for coordination/collaboration by state and federal agencies may provoke a response from service providers who form a nucleus group and ask others to join them. Regardless of the number of initial players, before the first meeting of any group, prepare them ahead of time. Send them information on the purpose of your meeting and request information from them about their previous experience, knowledge, and understanding of the issues around family literacy. The information contained in the "convening letter" should list:

1. The reasons for the meeting.
2. The desire to focus the right resources on solving the problem.

Choosing whom to invite to an initial meeting should be based on an understanding of which local agencies or organizations provide services to adult learners, children at risk, public and community schools, social service agencies, and the local library. Aim for a representative cross section of the community. Include, if possible, a leader of the business community or a company which employs a large numbers of people locally. A larger list of possible participants is suggested by reviewing partnerships formed by CCFL groups.

Prepare a questionnaire which asks potential partners to list their reasons for being represented or participating in a meeting and their concerns about becoming involved. This may also be done as an exercise if group members respond to individual questionnaires and indicate their interests on a sheet of newsprint to be discussed by the group later.

The questionnaire shown in Figure 4-1 may serve as a guide for the types of information that would be useful to gather before the first meeting.

TYPES OF PARTNERSHIPS

The following discussion of different types of partnerships or collaborative relationships is adapted from the work of Sally Habana-Hafner in her book *Partnerships for Community Development: Resources for Practitioners and Trainers* (University of Massachusetts, 1990). It is included here because it provides another way of looking at the complexities of the partnership process. Used as a handout, it may prove useful for a point of discussion early on in the development of a community collaboration.

When joining an organization, it is important to understand what type it is—public, private, or not-for-profit. As with single organizations, partnerships can be of different types. Each is useful and appropriate depending upon the purpose.

Networks, coordinations, or collaborations are three basic types or levels of partnerships that can be considered points on a continuum with varying differences in the following areas:

- Complexity of purposes—from simple information sharing to joint problem solving.
- Intensity of linkages—the degree to which they are linked together in their working relations and influenced by common goals, decision rules, shared tasks, and resources committed.
- Formality of agreements—the degree of formality among organizations concerns rules or agreements on operating structures, policies, and procedures.

Network Characteristics

Networks are often found at the state or corporate administrative level among similar information and service stakeholders. Organizations at the state, regional, or corporate level often form loose networks, meeting frequently to exchange information. The person who represents an entity in this partnership can easily either join or leave without having an effect on the network. The structural patterns of this type of network are generally informal. Most member organi-

---

FIGURE 4.1.   Community Questionnaire

Name: **Agency or Affiliation:**

Address: **Telephone:**

1. Do you think you will be able to attend or be represented at the meeting? (specify date)

2. Are you currently running any programs which, formally or informally, involve children and parents working and playing together? Please describe.

3. Are you currently providing educational services to parents? To adults? To children? Please describe.

4. Are you potentially interested in being involved—as a provider, planner, supporter, referral source, etc. in a family literacy program?

5. Do you have any ideas about particular groups of people who might be targets of such a program?

6. Do you have any ideas about how such a program might work, and/or who should be involved in its planning, set-up, implementation, and evaluation?

---

zations do not give up any separate autonomy to form the network. Sharing of resources is largely news, minutes, reports, messages, and so on. A statewide literacy coalition may be an example of a state partnership. Most of these networks do not require any separate physical space such as an office or building. An agency can be a member of many such networks without suffering a major commitment of its resources. This would be similar to the CCFL Level 3 (State or Corporate).

Coordination

Coordinating organizations are often found at the administrative level of community agencies. Organizations at the community level which begin working together may develop a more closely linked connection involving tasks that require resources other than information sharing. Membership is more stable, with considerable attention given to who joins and what happens if a member leaves. Process and structural patterns of the coordination are more formal, either verbal or written. Each member may agree to some loss of autonomy, with possible resulting effects on each member's patterns. Resource commitments involve some level of each member's assets—time, personnel, funds, or facilities. It is easier to *see* this type of partnership since its tasks or activities require more tangible processes and structures. (This type of group supports the work of the community collaboration and would designate a member of the organization to work at a more intense Level 2.)

Collaboration

Collaborations may involve a mixture of community agency directors and hopefully designated decision-making representatives. Member organization's collaborations are strongly linked and share a specific, often complex, and long range purpose. Membership is stable—adding or dropping members becomes a major issue and could result in significant changes in the partnership, perhaps even failure. Process and structural patterns are most often expressed in writing, often as legal documents (especially if co-funding is sought). Each member organization delegates considerable autonomy to the collaboration, with member representatives acting in the partnership with significant decision-making powers. Effects on each member organization's internal operations can be significant. The commitment of resources to this partnership can be quite heavy, requiring careful study before each organization decides to participate. A collaboration can be highly visible to others in the community or region and may even be more noticeable than any of the individual member organizations (parallel to CCFL Level 2).

Unmet needs may emerge from networks and coordinating groups as well and may also serve as brokers of vital information useful to the collaboration.

WHY GET INVOLVED
IN COLLABORATIONS?

Single organizations/agencies are formed in our communities in response to needs for particular services or products. Similarly, collaborations are formed for compelling needs which prompt community-based organizations to work together. There are both internal and external reasons to collaborate or form partnerships rather than networks or coordinating groups. Some reflect the following reasons:

1. Complex community problems

   No single organization has the capabilities to solve complex community problems. Many problems such as unemployment, housing, substance abuse, environmental pollution, and low literacy may be addressed more successfully by the work of community partnerships. The more organizations involved, the more resources available. When organizations find that they serve similar populations with similar needs, they may be able to meet the needs of their clients better through a shared approach.

2. Old Problems Need Fresh Solutions

   Different organizations can bring a fresh approach or a new way of looking at a problem. Broadening the perspective on a problem creates more chances to find better solutions. It offers an integrated approach to community problem solving.

3. Mandates from the Funders

   There is renewed emphasis from federal, state, and private funders which stresses cooperation and collaboration. With dwindling resources available, strong interorganizational relations eliminate duplication of efforts and maximize the use of existing resources. Funders view partnerships not only as a means for increasing the quality of service but also as a way to improve efficiency.

4. Desire for New Relationships

   Individuals in community-based organizations may want to build friendships outside their own setting, using their varied work-places as the context for getting together. Personal relations may develop into professional networks which may be rewarding and useful.

5. Public Relations Strategies

   All agencies, both public and private, need to promote a positive public image. As part of a public relations strategy, there is an increased interest in developing partnerships with other community organizations. Public agencies such as libraries gain new support and private organizations gain an image of being more "socially responsible". Everyone benefits from these new public/private partnerships.

6. Reduction in Resources

   Most programs are now suffering from dwindling resources. Public agencies are eliminating programs because of cuts in state and federal funding and the decreased assets of private foundations. Every year organizations are being challenged to do more with less. Organizations can creatively come together to share some program costs when serving the same groups.

7. Social, Economic and Political Agendas
   Organizations which are committed to social change feel that building coalitions, partnerships, action alliances, or collaborations will both strengthen and broaden their base of support. Action alliances are frequently motivated to jointly change the social, economic, and political structure of society towards a vision of a better world.

After examining the reasons for joining a collaboration, it may be helpful to have potential participants respond to these two central questions:

1. Which of the reasons listed may have motivated you or your agency to form a partnership?
2. Do you have other reasons for forming a partnership which are not included?

Be certain to check in on these questions as time passes to see how attitudes may have changed.

Step Two: Preparing and Conducting Effective Meetings

Due to the fact that time always seems so short, those who choose to develop a community collaboration and focus on a shared plan are frequently the most overworked people in their own jobs. As a result, it is important to make planning meetings as productive as possible. Collaborative groups which meet on a regular basis must design an organizational framework so that their meeting times run smoothly and focus on the mission of collaboration.

Based on previous experience in community organizing, the following suggestions may help make more effective use of your meeting time. Each group will be made of different representatives and some suggested techniques may not be equally appropriate for every collaboration. However, the following tips may prove helpful in making your meetings more successful.

- Draw up an agenda—The agenda will list the key issues to be discussed at each meeting, and at the end, you can set the agenda for the next time. Should members of the group wish to add agenda items, this can take place between meetings or the day of the meeting during *new business.*

- Review the agenda as a group—At the start of each meeting, review the agenda to see if items should be added or eliminated. At this time, the order of business can even be reconsidered. This provides an opportunity to discuss issues which may have come up between meetings.
- Assign a timeframe to each agenda item—Each agenda item should be considered in relationship to other issues. Members of any collaboration are busy people. By keeping to a set timeframe, the agenda will move along. You should assign a time limit for each item (e.g. forty-five minutes to discuss child care issues). If these limits are insufficient to fully explore the topic, you may choose to rearrange the agenda and eliminate another discussion item to allow more time for discussion or move the discussion topic into the next meeting, appointing a sub-committee to summarize the issues for a later report.
- List an outcome for the meeting—An outcome for each agenda item might be to make a firm decision about a given issue such as deciding on an appropriate site for a family literacy program. By listing outcomes, you will be aware that some progress is taking place, and it will move the decision-making process.
- Rotate a facilitator for each meeting—Collaborations are *most effective* when collegial leadership is practiced. By rotating the chair at each meeting no person is left with full responsibility for each meeting. Whoever acts as facilitator should negotiate any changes in the agenda when the group convenes and keep them focused on the tasks at hand. If the minute taking function is also rotated, everyone will have an opportunity to make a contribution to the group process. However, remember that not everyone is equally skilled at or desirous of being a facilitator.
- Decide how to make decisions—Decisions may be made by:
  1. Consensus (everyone comes to agreement),
  2. Democratic vote (majority rules),
  3. The group delegates one person to have the final word.
  The latter may be especially effective if the group needs to negotiate with a Level 3 state or corporate agency and one person must act as delegate or the representative of the group. Certain decisions will require different approaches. The group should agree on the process in advance to avoid any misunderstandings.
- Decide how group decisions will be remembered—Groups which work together over time, often forget how a decision was reached. When the discussion is especially long and heated, members of the collaboration may forget exactly how a specific decision was reached. Therefore consider the following options:
  1. Record decisions in the minutes of each meeting.
  2. Use newsprint to record decisions and transfer them to a specific *decisions* file or folder.
  3. Annotate the agenda as you go along indicating which and how decisions were made.

- Allow time for informal conversation—As members of the group meet with one another, an element of trust will begin to develop. Friendships will be formed and new relationships will evolve. Although the purpose of the meeting should be fixed on the agenda and tasks at hand, allowing some time for informal conversation will promote an atmosphere which promotes a team approach.
- Enjoy each others' company—Schedule some meetings as less formal "brown bag" lunches or devote another meeting to the shared task of stuffing envelopes for a community mailing where the only item of business is to get out information about the family literacy collaboration. Consider breaking into pairs or small groups to brainstorm an issue. Then reconvene as a group to discuss what you have discussed.
- Rotate your meeting sites—This is an excellent way to learn about the resources of each community agency. The host person may provide coffee, soft drinks, or snacks. Rotating the site does not place an undue burden on one organization.
- Periodically evaluate the effectiveness of the group process—This need not take place at every meeting, but from time to time the group should discuss how well they are working together. Allow time for specific suggestions about how to make the process smoother or bring up issues not covered on the regular agenda. A simple evaluation tool is the use of a sheet of newsprint with a two column list: "these things are working pretty well" and "these things need improvement." Short, constructive suggestions from the group on improving the process should go in the "improvement" column and provide the basis for some meaningful discussion.

FOCUSING ON THE PROBLEM: AN EXERCISE

While the first meeting may be more of an open-ended discussion about family literacy, members of the community collaboration should begin to focus in on the issue of literacy and define the problem first from their point of view moving eventually to a group or collaborative position in order to address the problem.

The following questions may serve as the basis for an initial discussion:

1. How is your organization affected by the impact of low literate families?
2. What do you see as the principal causes for the problem of intergenerational illiteracy?
3. Looking at the whole problem, what issues could reasonably be addressed by your agency or another community-based organization?

4. What resources do you currently offer which could address the family literacy issue, if even only in part?
5. What other resources are needed to alleviate this problem?
6. What is your agency's interest in getting involved in a partnership/collaborative approach?
7. What possible solutions could a number of agencies jointly develop to address family literacy within the community?
8. What would be some of the major objectives of a family literacy project?
9. What would be a realistic timeframe for such a project?

These questions would promote a structured discussion which would begin to clarify values, beliefs, and information within the group. A list of resources to be contributed by individual agencies/organizations could be generated. At this point, it is important to acknowledge the perspective and opinions of each member of the collaborative. These ideas should be considered in the proposed solution to a problem. It is important to maintain an open, accepting attitude during this process. Any point of conflict which may arise at this time should be dealt with. If the group can reach some consensus on an idea for a shared approach to a family literacy project, the collaboration will begin to move forward. If however, there is a great deal of disagreement, it may be appropriate to table the discussion and tackle some interim topics en route to the larger question.

The underlying principle of a successful collaboration is the articulation of a shared vision. In a word, the group must continue to focus on achieving a jointly developed, successful project. It is unrealistic to think that, given the diversity of organizations represented, individual members will immediately develop this shared vision. At this point, it might be important for individuals to talk about what would be an ideal goal to achieve for the coming year and within a few years. One of the most successful outcomes of planning is when the group sets a short-term goal which may be achieved within a brief period of time and which reinforces the concept of collaboration. This may be something as simple as a communications goal. For example, some may choose to brainstorm a name for their group or proposed project. A catchy project name such as the FLASH (Family Literacy Action Starts Here) program chosen by the Fitchburg, Massachusetts collaborative can be used in publicity, featured on brochures and press releases.

In most cases, after a number of focused meetings, the group will begin to come together cohesively. It is important to encourage members of the collaboration to maintain linkages with the staff at their regular worksite. For in fact, the intensity of what transpires within the collaboration may not be communicated well or even at all back to the supporting organization. Because of the time consuming nature of the community level collaboration, it is critical that the supporting agency understand that significant progress is taking place in this newly formed group.

Step Three: A Planning Process

In the course of developing a collaboration with a focus on family literacy several things will be taking place. First, your group will begin to take on an identity and as that identity shapes up, you will begin to focus on a workplan which will have a specific end.

As the group develops an identity, you should focus on:

1. Developing a working relationship among members of the groups.
2. Ensuring that each individual's agency will assist and support the organization.
3. Emphasizing the role and strengths of each agency in relation to the final outcome.
4. Promoting the most effective method of communication with both group members and their supporting agencies/staffs.

In order to develop a workplan for a family literacy project, the group must conduct a community assessment about the need for family literacy services in the community. Two available aids are Carole Talan's *Literacy Needs Assessment* or the *Literacy Kit Assessment, "Literacy Needs Resources"* adapted by United Way (see Appendix B). Both adult literacy and children's services in the community should be investigated.

A family literacy workplan should identify the aspect of the problem to be addressed by a possible project or program. It is important to note that though the needs will be many and may be great, it is important to focus on both specific short-term and long-term goals for a project.

Having identified the need, the group must come up with sound action plans or strategies to address the problem. Attention should be paid to the role and responsibilities and tasks of each person in the collaboration.

A thorough discussion of conducting a general needs assessment in preparation for writing any proposal is contained in the section on *Needs Assessment* in the following chapter on **Preparing for and Writing a Literacy Proposal**.

In order to adequately assess the community needs for family literacy services, the following questions need to be answered:

I. ASSESSING COMMUNITY NEED

1. What should be our working definition of family literacy?
2. Who has a need for family literacy services in your community?
3. How can you document this need (e.g. statistics on the poverty level, unemployment, number of persons on AFDC, literacy level of the community, number of children in Head Start/Chapter One)?

4. How can you locate these families? Are they in family shelters, housing projects, family clinics, etc.? (This can be determined by speaking with state and local welfare providers, local schools.)
5. What is the cultural background of these groups? Do they include linguistic minorities?
6. What kind of support services are needed to ensure participation? (Child care and transportation or even counseling may be among the most obvious services.)

II. IDENTIFYING RESOURCES

1. What organizations in the community address the literacy needs of parents and children? Adult education programs, school-based programs, workplace, Head Start, Chapter One?
2. What type of support services exist? Do state agencies provide a voucher system for housing or education?
3. Identify a list of key individuals, agencies, or organizations which may have resources. Use the chart of non-traditional data sources in the section on assessing the need in the proposal writing section. Generate a list of supporters to participate in a group exercise.
4. Identify the location of these resources in your community. Consider placing these as part of a community mapping exercise.
5. What other resources exist which could help address this need? Is outside funding from grants, adult education, library, workforce available?

III. BRIDGING THE GAP BETWEEN SERVICES AND RESOURSES

1. What is the impact of social and political events, and economic cuts (both positive and negative) on the problem?
2. What is the current climate of cooperation within the community?
3. Identify some successful cooperative ventures among agencies.

The following three exercises adapted from Habana-Hafner are valuable for collaborative members to work on as a group. Plan to spend about thirty minutes on the first exercise, *Identifying Key Individuals and Settings*. This will suggest what organizations/persons may have an influence on the development of a collaborative family literacy project. You may make a copy of this exercise for each member to work on individually, or using a large sheet of newsprint, brainstorm in a group session. Your group may choose to do any of the following exercises more than once.

FIGURE 4.2.   Collaborative Exercise 1: Assessing the Community

IDENTIFYING KEY INDIVIDUALS AND SETTINGS

As a group, take about 20 minutes to identify the key settings such as neighbor-hoods, groups, organizations and individuals as politicians, community leaders, constituents, and stakeholders in your community environment. Indicate if they are a direct or indirect influence on the issue of family literacy. This may provide an initial list of potential members to approach to join your partnership.

Who/What	Direct Influence	Indirect Influence

SETTINGS:

Neighborhoods _____   _____   _____

Local Schools _____   _____   _____

Local Government _____   _____   _____

Public Agencies _____   _____   _____

Foundations _____   _____   _____

Community Based
Organizations _____   _____   _____

Interest Groups _____   _____   _____

Worksites _____   _____   _____

Similar Partnerships _____   _____   _____

Other _____   _____   _____

INDIVIDUALS:

Key Private Individuals _____   _____   _____

Agency Directors _____   _____   _____

Community Leaders _____   _____   _____

Constituents _____   _____   _____

Local Gov. Officials _____   _____   _____

FIGURE 4.3.   Collaborative Exercise 2: Force Field Analysis

As a group, use the sheet below to identify those influences which have either a positive or negative impact upon the literacy needs of the community. Using the list below, or other appropriate terms, write down the *helping* or positive forces and the *hindering* or negative forces which will prevent a successful collaboration. Make every attempt to generate terms which are **specific** to your community. This exercise can be done by providing a photocopy of this sheet to everyone in the group or by using this sheet as a model and brainstorming the helping and hindering forces on a large sheet of newsprint.

Terms to consider:

physical conditions   economic trends   political climate
national priorities   material resources   human resources

Positive or Helping Forces   **Negative or Hindering Forces**

_____   _____

_____   _____

_____   _____

_____   _____

_____   _____

_____   _____

Based on this list, try to think of a number of strategies to deal with the hindering forces or a strategy to strengthen the helping forces.

1. Strategy: _____

2. Strategy: _____

3. Strategy: _____

FIGURE 4.4.   Collaborative Exercise 3: Community Mapping

After you have gone through the previous exercises of identifying key individuals and the force field analysis use this information to design a map of your community. On a large piece of newsprint or a sheet of paper, draw a physical map of your community. Add the various forces (social, political, economic, etc.) which will have an impact on your community.

Be creative with your ideas. Think of how you could best describe your community from MANY different perspectives. This is best done as a group exercise. If the group comes from many communities an ''ideal'' community can serve as the stimulus.

KEY SYMBOLS:

Physical:
schools, adult learning centers, library (and branches) community based organizations, housing projects, parks, freeways and other topographical barriers and features, key businesses e.g. factories, etc.

Social:
low income, middle class, affluent, upper-class, working class/ pink and blue collared, ethnic ''barrios'' Latino, Southeast Asian, Chinese, African American communities, etc.

Economic:
business district, downtown, industrial community, low income neighborhoods, malls, etc.

Other influences: make up symbols to describe other forces e.g.new waves of immigrants, shut down of local factory, cutbacks in state aid, etc.

Consider the impact of:

Physical elements—Boundaries of city, town, freeways, topography, natural resources. How do these boundaries isolate groups from services? Chart where adult/children's services are provided in relation to where these groups live and work.

Demographics—Number of people, characteristics of varied groups, family patterns, social status, affiliation to other groups, educational status, immigration patterns.

Community background—Relate the story of the region: rural, traditional farming, urban spilling into suburbs; national, political and economic conditions; possible support or resistance from the above.

Community groups—Social class, ethnic differences, traditions, role of women, youth, and the ''poor.''

FIGURE 4.4 (cont).   A Family Literacy Collaboration for Our Town, USA

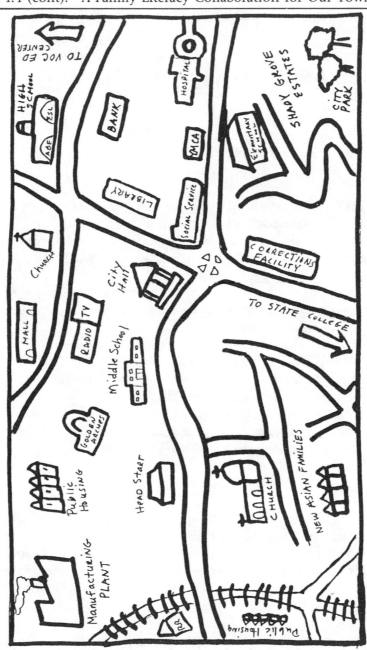

TEAM INSTRUCTIONS:
1. Choose agencies and design a family literacy collaboration for our town
2. List three advantages of collaboration with each agency
3. Identify three barriers and solutions to the collaboration
4. Identify three objectives for the first meeting

Having completed and utilized these exercises, a gap in services will begin to emerge and the group will be pointed in a direction of solutions to close the gap.

Step Four: Developing Shared Project Ideas

The group must consider the following questions in the development of a shared project:

1. What activities should take place to meet the stated purpose and objectives? What is the focus of the project?
2. Based on the four generic types of family and intergenerational literacy programs (Fig.1-1), what approach will you take for a shared project? What type is feasible in your community?
3. What existing resources do individual agencies have to begin or continue these activities? The group may decide to generate a list of resources, agencies, and contact people.
4. What activities are currently being offered in your community and how could they relate to your proposed project?
5. Based on a list of potential activities, select those most appropriate to meet the proposed project goals and objectives.
6. Given the timeframe for the proposed project, determine which of the activities can be targeted for implementation.
7. What new resources (personnel, materials, space, equipment) are needed to carry out these activities?
8. How will a project be evaluated?

In order to come to consensus about a project idea, begin by brainstorming a list of possible solutions or approaches on newsprint.

Review ideas, revise, consolidate, and decide what is the most important priority for a project. Try to reach a consensus as a group to determine the scope of the project. Decide who will be the primary person(s) responsible for writing or developing a project proposal.

SOME HELPFUL TIPS STEPS ON REACHING CONSENSUS

- Ask individual people to present information relevant to making a decision and identify someone to collect statistics on high school drop-out rate, number of families on AFDC, etc.

- Allow enough time to discuss an issue, and do not be pressured into making a quick decision. Assign a specific amount of time for discussion, and if you cannot reach a decision agree to postpone it until the next meeting with a specific result in mind.
- Be sensitive to the fact that not all members of the group are equally comfortable in verbal exchanges.
- Avoid arguing your point of view and give time for a response by listening.
- Don't use tactics such as flipping a coin or majority rules, keep on working at consensus. Sometimes if people are willing to give up a little on both sides they may be happier if not coerced into agreement.
- Don't avoid conflict or withdraw a suggestion because you are concerned about conflict.
- Always look for common ground. Try to find a point where you agree with someone and work from there.*

*Biagi, R., *Working Together: A Manual for Helping Groups Work More Effectively, Citizen Training Project,* (Consensus Building) University of Massachusetts: Amherst, MA 1978

SUSTAINING INVOLVEMENT WITH THE COMMUNITY

Once your collaboration has begun to make progress on the group's *shared vision,* it is important to consider information from community organizations and individuals as input into the active project design.

Some of the following ideas may be successful in enlisting community support:

1. Set up meetings with individuals and organizations identified on *force field analysis* chart to get feed back on potential project design.
2. Develop a concept paper for a shared project idea and distribute it to community groups with potential interest in supporting the needs of families.
3. Share the concept paper for the project idea with staff members of collaboration partners to get a reaction to the proposed project design.
4. Involve adult learners/parents in the design of the project. (Note: many adult learners prefer the term "family learning" when used to describe an actual program.)

Having built a community collaboration and developed a project design, it would be an appropriate next step for the group to seek outside funding to turn their *shared vision* into a real family literacy program.

Six Profiles

Three of the following six communities were funded as part of the Community Collaborations for Family Literacy Project using LSCA Title I monies for the 1992-93 fiscal year. Three other libraries represent communities which developed a family literacy program in collaboration with local agencies and organizations. All may serve as potential models for replication for other library-based family literacy projects.

The Fitchburg Public Library: Family Literacy Action Starts Here (FLASH)

Funding: LSCA Title I $25,000 and LSCA Title VI $35,000.

After receiving LSCA Title I funds from the Massachusetts Board of Library Commissioners to implement the program in Fitchburg, Elizabeth Watson, director of the Fitchburg Public Library, was successful in securing additional funds under LSCA Title VI to expand the program to include the communities of Gardner and Leominster. In the fall of 1992, she hired project coordinator, Cathy Apfel, who was given the responsibility of coordinating instructional programs for adults, providing for child care, and designing children's activities in the three communities. Cathy met with vendors to explore the purchase of appropriate teaching resources for a Family Resource Center. Flyers with appropriate program information were designed and distributed to local service agencies, adult education centers, and childcare agencies. Information also appeared in the local newspaper and on cable television. A meeting with WGBH, about the Boston-based public broadcasting station's Family Literacy Alliance, resulted in the designation of the FLASH program as a project site. This relationship will provide VHS tapes of Reading Rainbow, Wonderworks, and Long Ago and Far Away—books, materials, and training for the project staff. Classes are held at Head Start facilities in two communities and at Mount Wachusett Community College in a third. Six months into the project, fifteen families are actively participating on Wednesday and Friday afternoons. Adults receive instruction in functional reading, writing, and communication skills. Children are involved in story reading conducted by the children's librarian with follow-up activities. Intergenerational activities and special events take place every Wednesday afternoon.

Cathy Apfel comments that she has been somewhat discouraged by the attendance rate which has averaged about 50 percent, however, the weather has been a critical factor this winter and illness and lack of transportation have contributed to the problem. The library will provide vouchers to families to cover transportation costs which should improve attendance. Library staff have introduced parents and children to the bilingual collection and all children have been registered for a library card.

Wareham Public Library: Family Learning Center

Funding: LSCA Title I $25,000

The Wareham Free Library's Family Learning Center is being offered as an extension of, and in coordination with, services offered by the Wareham Chapter One, Even Start, local Head Start, and Wareham Adult Basic Education. Library Director, Mary Jane Pillsbury designed a program which includes the following components:

- Direct service to adults which focus on reading.
- Writing and parenting skills.
- Parent-child activities.
- Adult literacy tutoring and workshops on parenting, child development, and advocacy.

Library activities are coordinated by Susan Pizzaletto, the Family Learning Center Coordinator. The program utilizes computers and software to develop the literacy skills of the whole family.

In the fall, a designated area in the children's room was set up as the Family Learning Center. Two computers are located in the area which houses the family learning collection. All selections and program objectives are reviewed by the community collaborative.

The project coordinator and children's librarian meet daily to plan out story hours which are held on Mondays and Thursdays. They have made every effort to select stories with a strong narrative and simple illustrations which allow interaction and questions from the children. Because of fluctuations in the group, such as new families coming in every week, it was decided to recruit volunteers to read to some children on a one-on-one basis. After several months of story-hours, project staffmembers noticed an improvement in the children's attention span. Many can now sit still for a longer time and discuss characters and stories. It was also observed that many parents were initially punitive when their children misbehaved. Some would grab the child, place a hand over his or her mouth, restrain or even wrestle the child to the floor. It was obvious to project staff that parents need to meet together in the classroom to discuss what happens during a story hour and what behaviors to encourage. Take home activities accompany every story time. A parent-child craft which extends the story goes home with a family and teachers report that children enjoy doing the activities at home.

The Somerville Public Library: Building Lifelong Readers

Funding: LSCA Title I $19,518

The Somerville Public Library chose to emphasize the library support role for family literacy in their community. Direct instruction for low-literate families is provided by a local Adult Learning Center, Project SCALE, and by a federally-funded Even Start grant to the schools. Project Director, Ann Dausch, hired a family literacy coordinator who has the responsibility for developing a collection of family literacy materials to be housed in a special area of the library. A series of thematic kits for take-home use were developed and family storyhours and programming appropriate to the target group has been ongoing. Arrangements have been made to enable Even Start staff to accompany the project coordinator to parks and housing projects on the library's bookmobile in order to provide summer programming for members of the target group. The library set up a dial-a-story line which has been an instant success. Several prominent Somerville residents, including the Mayor, have offered to record the "story of the week."

The Project Coordinator, a professional librarian with a background in early childhood education, was hired. The Family Reading Room was equipped with preschool toys, a child's table, chairs, filing cases of craft materials, and equipment to support the project. The coordinator has developed a series of story hour kits for low literate families to borrow and use at home. A series of five workshops have been scheduled to take place both at the library and at local housing projects. Project topics include "How to Choose Books for Children" and "How to Tell Stories to Your Child."

The members of the community collaboration who were so instrumental in supporting this project have been meeting on a monthly basis and will be designing a joint family literacy celebration in May. This project continues to enjoy wide support from literacy providers in the community and the family literacy coordinator, Sydelle Pearl, has been successful in networking with the many community agencies.

Morrill Memorial Library, Norwood, MA Family Learning Project

Funding: LSCA Title I $24,650

The Morrill Memorial Library's family literacy project is an outgrowth of the library's successful volunteer adult literacy program. Literacy Coordinator, Bettina Blood, developed a family project which expands to focus on the literacy needs of the entire family and provides opportunities for parents to become partners in their children's education.

The library established a child drop-in center staffed by trained volunteers who provided individual or small-group activities for children while their parents were being tutored in the library's literacy program. Family book sharing sessions and parent workshops are designed to prepare parents to extend the print environment into their home activities.

This project was guided by a twelve-member community advisory committee which decided upon the project name "LIFT," an acronym for Learning Involves Families Together. Press releases describing the program were sent to seven local newspapers and a special brochure was printed which described the services available through the program. Twelve families have been actively involved with this program and more have been recruited for the spring. These families all have small children with either the mother or father currently receiving literacy services through the Literacy Volunteers affiliated program.

The library utilizes computers for adult literacy instruction and has begun to introduce computer activities to parents. The library programs continue to attract large numbers of participants with such topics as "On the Spot Games that Teach Reading, Language and Thinking" and "Writing Family Stories."

Public Service Announcements (PSA's) were shown over the local cable television station and the project coordinator was a guest on local talk radio. The medium of television and radio continues to be an effective method of recruitment. Because the library's literacy program has been well established it has been easier to incorporate the family learning center components into regular activities.

Palmer Public Library "New Visions for New Learners"

Funding: LSCA Title I $14,300

The Palmer Public Library, which has maintained a viable volunteer literacy program affiliated with Literacy Volunteers, chose to follow a model developed by the Vermont Council of the Humanities which utilized children's literature as a link between new learners and their children. The Vermont project is centered around a reading and discussion series on the themes of American History, Other Cultures, and Family Relationships. The program involves new learners, adult literacy tutors, a project coordinator, and a scholar/facilitator. Through the reading and discussion of children's literature and the enjoyment of puppeteers and storytellers, new learners, their children, and their grandchildren are introduced to the joys of reading.

Library Director Olga Holmberg hired Robin Kline as the program coordinator to direct all project activities. The New Visions program also worked with local GED teachers reaching out to learners in surrounding communities. Additionally, the coordinator made presentations at both elementary and middle school PTA meetings and to senior citizens groups in an effort to expand community awareness about the project.

The three discussion series begin with an introductory session and a tour of the library for participants. Each series includes four one-and-one-half hour sessions with a fifth session scheduled at the end of the program as a family event. It is open to participants' children and grandchildren and features either a storyteller or puppeteer. Free child care for the program is provided by four volunteers in the children's section of the library. All books read for the program become the property of the new learner. Publicity includes bookmarks with reading lists appropriate to the theme and reading level of new readers and a handout sheet including *Tips for Tutors and Parents and Kids Reading Together.*

Thirty people, including 15 adult learners and 15 tutors, attended the first discussion session. The initial response to this program has been slow although many tutors were personally contacted about the goals and purpose of the New Visions program. However, participant attendance has been steady as new learners return to each session expressing a comfort level with the scholar/facilitator and the rest of the group. For example, many learners appeared eager to discuss the issues of adoption which were raised in such titles as *The Great Gilly Hopkins,* by Katherine Paterson. After the first two sessions, the evaluations revealed that 65 percent of learners were able to read all four books. Everyone found the discussions lively and interesting. It was anticipated that some books would be a challenge to participants. Most of all, it was heartening to see students follow the suggestions of the facilitator and many are now reading the program books to their children. Library staffmembers are assured that the program has been quite effective in expanding an interest in children's literature among new learners. This excitement seems to extend to the children of participants. In the latest survey, eleven of twelve people responding to a simple evaluation form revealed that they had shared the discussion books with their children/ grandchildren.

This approach to family literacy builds upon an instructional program which was already established within the library. It provides model activities for the parent and shared literacy events for children and parents at the end of each session.

Plymouth Public Library: Family Literacy Workshop
Plymouth, MA

Funding: State funds from the Commonwealth Inservice Institute

Mary Ann O'Dell, Director of the Plymouth Library Literacy Program, received a special Commonwealth Inservice Institute Grant from the state to offer a series of parenting workshops to low income parents. Workshop sessions were open to participants with children in Head Start, including those characterized as "at risk." Some, but not all, parents were receiving literacy instruction through the library's literacy program.

The program was not styled as a full service family literacy project, but rather as a *Family Literacy Workshop Series* which provided training on how parents could become reading partners with their children. The series of seven workshops ran approximately two hours per session and included topics on:

- TV or not TV
- Reading Aloud
- Developing Family Games
- Storytelling
- Special Needs
- Early Childhood Development
- Childhood Nutrition

All presenters focused on the need for literacy when performing tasks such as reading food labels or selecting a program from the television guide. The session on childhood nutrition stressed the importance of dealing with problem eaters and provided valuable information about the new guidelines on fat and cholesterol from the Food and Drug Administration.

Most parents responded to an evaluation form with positive comments and surprised staff by suggesting that the workshops run even longer than the two hours.

The session on making games was based on the story of *The Little Engine That Could.* Parents were delighted with the opportunity to make a game based on this favorite childhood story using low cost materials such as manila folders, spinners, and magic markers. Parents were encouraged to read this story to their children and then play the game with them.

The programs were all held in the literacy center at the library. The children's librarian presented a session on reading aloud to children and introduced participants to an enticing array of books to check out. All parents were registered for a library card and given an introduction to other library services.

Although the current emphasis is more on parenting for low-income parents, the Plymouth Library Literacy program is seeking to expand this program into a full family literacy program by writing a joint proposal with community representatives of Chapter One and a local teen parenting program. The library would also like to offer pre-GED and GED classes as part of the library's literacy program and coordinate with early childhood providers to offer classes for participants' children. The Family Literacy Workshop classes would continue as part of this expanded program.

SECTION THREE

5
WRITING A LITERACY PROPOSAL

Overview

Given a new federal priority for literacy under the National Literacy Act and the Library Services and Construction Act (Titles I and VI) more money is currently available for program development than in any period in recent history. Libraries and community agencies seeking to serve low literate populations will be able to access these and other resources if they understand the mechanics of writing a successful proposal.

With the passage of the National Literacy Act, public libraries, literacy organizations and community coalitions may receive funding for such things as:

1. Establishing a new program or service (either volunteer or classroom-based).
2. Adding a new training component such as computer-assisted instruction.
3. Expanding to include writing programs for adult learners.
4. Developing a family literacy component which deals with the needs of the children of educationally disadvantaged learners.

Preparation for project development should be grounded in the planning efforts of the library with collaborating community agencies to meet the real needs of the identified target population. Unfortunately, library and other organizations sometimes decide to apply for money for literacy simply because it is available. Sometimes two agencies discover literacy is a priority of funding sources and a decision is made to apply for funds. However, with this new emphasis on preparation and planning, agency or library staff are well served in taking the necessary steps to meet community needs together. In all cases, a proposed project should be decided upon and agreed to by all agencies involved and based on the priorities of needs to be addressed. Alternatively, the planning steps outlined under the community collaboration planning agenda, which draws various members of the community together, can also serve as a forum to generate ideas that can be developed into a sound proposal.

There are two approaches to achieving agreed outcomes for service. An idea may be developed without a clear indication of how it will be funded, or before a funding source with matching priorities is located. Writing a proposal follows a fairly standard format whether the request is submitted to the Barbara Bush Foundation for Family Literacy or to the National Institute for Literacy.

Many foundations, such as Toyota Family Literacy, the Barbara Bush Foundation, as well as state libraries and adult education agencies, provide prospective proposal writers with a Request for Proposals, referred to as the RFP. This may include a standard application which should be strictly followed, especially as to the format, number of pages (usually around 20, double spaced), and any required attachments.

When the funding source does not provide an application, the proposal writer should use a format based on the standard elements of the proposal and the funder's stated criteria.

Finding a Funding Source

It is important to review the funder's guidelines to determine if the proposed project will meet the funding priorities of the foundation or chosen government agency. A number of regional grant centers across the country provide resources for additional re-search. A number of foundations or corporations such as Bell Atlantic or local banks and businesses actually seek to fund discrete geographic areas and counties. It is important to check the size of the average award made by these foundations over the last three to five years. Should a literacy program require an annual income of $20,000, a typical foundation that ordinarily gives an average award of $5,000 will not sustain a program unless combined with other funding. The timeline of applying for a grant is critical. Identify due dates and be alert to funding cycles. If current project funding expires in October, for example, program staff should attempt to secure funding at least eight months in advance. Decisions may occur once a year, twice a year, or even quarterly. Finally, it is imperative to pursue a variety of funding sources with the same criteria.

When requesting funds from a foundation/agency it may be necessary to send a letter of inquiry. It is at this point that some agencies will send off a *concept paper* which includes a brief project description and a proposed budget figure to ascertain interest from a potential funder.

Writing the Proposal

Proposal writing is a skill not usually taught in school, but more frequently learned on the job. The good news is that the more you write, the better you get at it. The best news is that you can learn a lot by reading successfully funded proposals. For novice proposal writers it may be helpful to request a copy of a successfully funded proposal as a guideline. State library or adult education departments should be willing to provide an example of a successfully funded proposal on request.

Make a strong statement about your group's track record and how much you have been able to accomplish already. Let the facts speak for themselves and convince the reader that your organization is in the best position to carry out such a project. Use positive, expressive, action-oriented statements instead of passive, vague language.

Proposal development that is the outgrowth of an idea developed by a group can be very effective. However, writing the final proposal is best left to one or two people at most. All those with a vested interest in the project outcome (agency staff members, advisory board, other community collaborators) should be invited to read and react to the final draft. If you spend the necessary time, talent, and energy laying the groundwork, you will be well served in the end with a successful proposal which will provide valuable resources for your community.

KEY QUESTIONS TO ANSWER IN A PROPOSAL

Ordinarily, the proposal answers the following key questions:

- Why is this project needed at this time?
- What do you plan to do for the target population? State goals clearly (plan of service, measures of effectiveness).
- What kind of personnel will be required to implement the project?
- Why is your agency/library/collaborative group the best organization to handle the proposed project? What are the unique talents, experiences, or skills your group offers the project?
- What expertise/knowledge/understanding of the target group do you have to make this a successful project?
- What other organizations are working together on this project? Who are the members of the community collaboration?
- How will you know if the project has been successful? Specify your evaluation plan.
- How much of the total operation costs of this project is sought by this proposal?

Funding opportunities emerge over time or may present themselves on very short notice. Active proposal writers frequently maintain general information about their community and statistics about the groups they serve in a computer file often referred to as *the boilerplate.* While a standardized format may provide a useful framework, successful writers will tailor and specify their requests to the funder's guidelines.

There are several key elements you should remember in either case:

1. You determine that the funder's application fits your priorities.
2. Collect data within and beyond your program which both support target group needs and project trends.
3. Maintain watchfulness of funding sources by accessing source documents such as the Federal Register and by using a Regional Granstmanship Center.
4. Rely on word of mouth and sharing among local collaborators to identify potential sources.
5. Continually promote the visibility and value of your program.
6. Keep one or more draft outlines of desired project proposals on hand ready for funding opportunities. Deadlines are often short—two or three weeks.

THE BOILERPLATE

Proposal writing can be time consuming—especially when it is your first undertaking. However, by maintaining statistics and information in a computer file, you will facilitate the process of writing any new or revised proposal. Periodically you should update all general information on community needs or problems in order to take advantage of potential funding opportunities. Following the standard format regarding the elements of a proposal, you can maintain a file of information on many of the standard categories which will facilitate writing the finished proposal.

The *Elements of a Proposal* section that follows discusses each element of the proposal writing process in more detail and how best to prepare a winning proposal application.

A key to securing funds is a careful examination of the criteria and requirements of the funding source. For example, you may be asked to provide the per capita income rate of unemployment in your area. The proposal writer must carefully describe how the needs of the community and target population fit the priorities established by the funding source. It is important to outline a plan of operation which clearly describes the needs of the population, overarching goals, objectives and activities, and an explanation of how the project will be evaluated.

Elements of a Proposal

1. Letter of introduction or transmittal
2. Title Page
3. Project Abstract
4. Table of Contents
5. Introduction To the Proposal
6. Statement of Need
7. Project Design
8. Budget and Narrative
9. Agency capabilities/statement of capacity
10. Evaluation
11. Key Personnel
12. Cooperation/collaboration (letters of support may be requested)
13. Appendixes

You can use the standard elements of a proposal as a model when constructing your application. Here is where the writing process begins:

1. LETTER OF INTRODUCTION OR TRANSMITTAL

This letter accompanies most grant proposals. It provides a brief, first-time introduction to the funder about your agency and your project. Although not required by every funding source, the introductory letter is an effective tool to launch your request for support.

2. TITLE PAGE

Many funding agencies supply a standardized title page which must be filled out. For example, all federal proposal applications include a sheet, "Application for Federal Assistance" which includes pre-printed information like the CFDA (Catalog for Federal Domestic Assistance) number and the closing date when proposals are due. This page begins all proposals if a pre-printed title page is used—it will be the first page of your proposal. Otherwise, the abstract page which follows will include much of the same information.

Choose a title for your proposal which captures the essence of your project. For example two Massachusetts library projects are: The FLASH Program: (Family Literacy Action Starts Here) or the FLIP Project (Family Literacy Program in Marlboro/Hudson). One program which works with inmate mothers is called MotherRead. Another program is called Parents and Children Together (PACT). The idea is to capture your program in words more compelling than a non-descriptive title such as "The New Town Library Family Literacy Program." This sounds like the title of every other family literacy program in the country. Remember that many adult learners prefer the use of the words "family learning" for their programs.

3. ABSTRACT

After the title page, include a sheet which lists the name of your agency/library, address, telephone number, contact person, and amount of funds requested. This should be followed by a brief summary of your project in one hundred words or less. This section should excite the reader about what is special and unique in your project. The abstract is frequently used by funding agencies to determine the appropriateness of a proposal and to match your request with their funding priorities.

In any typical public or private response cycle, hundreds of applications are received. Funders may attempt to match requests for funds with the expertise of their proposal readers. *It is best to compose the abstract when you have finished writing the final draft of your proposal when all thematic ideas are clear and organized.*

4. TABLE OF CONTENTS

After the proposal is completely finished, go back and note the order of presentation of each section in the proposal. The table of contents enables the reader to go back and review areas in the proposal such as the budget section without searching through many pages. It shows organization and indicates your capability in managing a project.

5. INTRODUCTION

This section may be a simple short overview of your agency/organization and the project which you propose. In this segment, call attention to some unique aspect of the project or the approach which you plan to take. It sets the reader up for the case which you will make in the needs section which follows.

6. STATEMENT OF NEED

The statement of need is the part of the proposal where you will make a compelling argument for why your project should be funded. You must convince the reader of the importance of this project. Here you will describe the target group and clearly define the problem. Begin by stressing that illiteracy is a national problem of many dimensions, supporting your statement with the latest and most local statistics. You may also compare your community's literacy level with that of other counties, cities, or regions. Demonstrate the impact of illiteracy on your local community. For example, an important and much discussed issue today is the skill level of the current workforce. Federal, state, and regional Private Industry Councils are paying particular attention to displaced factory workers now replaced by technology. These people need serious retraining and many cannot function at higher level skills jobs because of their poor literacy levels; so discuss the need in human terms. For example, stress that parents in the target group are unable to make the best decisions to help their children because of their literacy deficiencies. This is where you make a strong case for early intervention for pre-schoolers and cite studies about the importance of early learning. By humanizing the need, you will bring the situation home to the reader.

There are usually two ways people become aware of a situation of need—it is either a clearly evident need in the community or it is a latent need that becomes apparent when local social workers are consulted.

In the obvious situation, critical incidents may take place so that community agencies, personnel, or library staff become aware of the need. They may receive many phone calls requesting material to help someone else learn how to read. Staff in community agencies may respond to concerns raised by adult learners about their children's education. In this case, an agency which already offers a literacy program, may choose to write a proposal to increase capacity (services) or add a family literacy component. With the need to increase services, it would be important to build your case for more or different services by citing various and specific data, (e.g. long waiting lists for your program).

If the problem is latent in the community, one may infer there is a need by reading newspaper articles about the presence of a problem or directly from service providers who work with members of the target group. These workers may mention the problems confronted by parents who are also adult learners.

Documenting the Need

Use both national and local sources of data to document the need. Include statistics from your local schools. Ask yourself the following questions:

- Does an adult education/GED program exist in the community?
- How many learners are being served? Where do they come from?
- Have local colleges/institutes identified special educational concerns in their communities?

Another source of accurate data is available from the 1990 census. Many community development agencies in cities and regions are involved in long-range planning for their regions. County systems such as Local Rapid Transit frequently publish studies which include information on employment and training. State Departments of Labor maintain statistics on the numbers of workers who require retraining. It is advisable to maintain an up-to-date clip file of current information in the course of the year and refer to this data as you write your statement of need.

Community Demographics Sources

U.S. Department of Commerce
United States Bureau of the Census
Federal Office Building No. 3
Suitland and Silver Hills, Suitland, MD 20233
(301) 763-4100

The Census Bureau provides publications through Government Depository Libraries and State Data Center Affiliates. These publications are available through the U.S. Government Printing Office. Examples of some Census publications which are useful to support a statement of need are:

- *1990 Census of Housing: General Housing Characteristics*
- *1990 Census of Population: General Population Characteristics for each State and General Social and Economic Characteristics*
- *County and City Data Book* (current edition)
- *State and Metropolitan Data Book* (current edition)

State Data Centers: State Data Centers are located in every state. Contact the United States Department of Commerce or individual State Libraries for the address of the State Data Center.

Each state publishes demographic statistics in conjunction with the U.S. Census Bureau. Each state center maintains a special collection of state census publications. In addition, they may conduct surveys with a specific regional emphasis.

United States Department of Education
Office of Educational Research and Improvement
400 Maryland Ave. SW
Washington, DC 20202-7240

Statistics on Adult Education/Literacy can be obtained from the following address:

National Center for Education Statistics
555 New Jersey Ave. NW
Washington, D.C. 20208
(202) 219-2000.

This Department collects information on research, statistics, and demonstration projects.

All federally administered library programs are located at this address. Information on Title VI programs is available from this office.

In addition, each individual State Department of Education has a Bureau of Data collection which maintains:

- School enrollment figures by municipality
- School enrollment figures for race and language by municipality

State Department of Employment and Training: Most state employment and training office's collect:

- Employment statistics for every municipality
- Workforce statistics by state
- Payroll and industry statistics for each state municipality.

The Department of Labor maintains the Bureau of Labor Statistics Regional Offices in the following cities: Boston, New York, Philadelphia, Atlanta, Chicago, Dallas, Kansas City, MO, and San Francisco.

Additonal sources of data include:

- Regional Planning Agencies
- State Department of Elder Affairs
- State Office of Handicapped Affairs
- State Office for Children
- Local Town Clerk's Offices
- Local School District Offices.

As you explore the problem, identify the local service providers and the types of services offered. In addition to the more traditional adult education providers, consider making contact with some of the community agencies that deal with the day-to-day survival problems of the target group. For example, the local health department or community agencies such as the Woman's, Infants, and Children's (WIC) program may have a better understanding of the needs of families who live with crisis.

The following agencies/organizations can be considered valuable partners in a community collaboration and can also provide you with information about the target population to support the statement of need.

Non-Traditional Data Sources

- Head Start
- Day Care Providers
- Literacy Volunteers
- Health Department
- Local Hospital
- Chapter One/School
- Housing Projects
- Local/ State literacy coalitions
- YMCA/YWCA
- Library Resource Center
- Student Literacy Corps.
- Community College
- Educational foundations
- Teen Parenting Program
- Local Service Clubs (Rotary, Lions)

- WIC (Woman, infants children) program
- Bookmobile
- Multicultural Service Agencies
- Ethnic clubs and organizations
- State Legislators
- Local Merchants/Welcome Wagon
- City/County Jail/Correctional Institution
- Congressmen/women
- Family/woman's shelter
- Drug and alcohol rehabilitation
- Mental Health Centers
- Halfway Houses/Soup Kitchens
- Newspapers/reporters
- Cable Television/Radio Stations
- Council on Aging
- Churches/synagogues/mosques
- League of Women voters
- Community Schools
- Public Health Centers
- Continuing Education Programs in Community Schools
- Police/Fire Department/Post Office Workers
- Chamber of Commerce/ Town Clerk
- Family Planning Clinics
- Recreation Centers/ Youth Clubs
- Goodwill Industries/Salvation Army
- Department of Motor Vehicles
- Employment and Training Centers

The needs assessment under development should relate directly to the mission of your agency/library. It is important to demonstrate a commitment to the target group. Your organization's history of working with families or adults in need of literacy training should be highlighted in this section of the proposal. If this is a new project or service, it is important to document your track record or past experience in providing outreach to a previously underserved population. Most proposals should be client centered. In other words, instead of identifying the library's lack of an adult new reader collection, the writer should focus on the importance of providing all patrons access to material at an appropriate reading level for their informational, recreational, and educational needs. Instead of simply stating that there is no family literacy program in the community, the writer should focus on the significant problems faced by parents who do not communicate with their child's school because they lack the reading skills and confidence to meet with the teachers. Dwell on the need to break the cycle of family illiteracy. By building the case for a new or expanded project based on human, not institutional needs, you will have engaged the reader and advanced your chances for funding.

The Statement of Need will:

- Describe the target population (including their characteristics and number).
- Be supported by statistics from reliable local, regional, and national sources using correct citations.
- Name the target group's most critical needs, indicating why this project meets a priority among those needs. Be specific.
- Indicate how those specific needs are addressed in the proposal.
- Discuss why those specific needs are currently not being met.
- Include input from the target population and from people experienced in providing service to the group.
- Be stated in terms of the client's needs, not in terms of an agency's or library's lack of services.

When the draft of this section is completed, the statement of need should also answer the following questions:

- Is this project clearly related to your agency/library's planning initiatives? Does it tie in with the organization's mission and goals?
- Is it supported by evidence drawn from a history and experience with the target group and is it documented by statistics?
- Does the statement answer which people have the need and how many are within the geographic area needing service? What percentage of the total population does this represent? Don't exaggerate the number.
- Does it introduce the solution—a family literacy program—as a clear response to community needs?
- Is this project one which can be reasonably accomplished within a realistic time period, say twelve months?
- Is the project stated in terms of the clients' needs, not the library or agency's needs?
- What has been done thus far to help this group by either the library or other community agencies? What services are currently available?
- Why is the proposed solution needed at this time?
- How will this project affect not only the target group but others in the community and staff and community agency members?

There are several assessment instruments which can be used when collecting information to make competent and informed decisions which support your case for funding.

Five Assessment Instruments To Measure Community Need

There are five types of needs assessment instruments which you can use to better understand and document target group needs. They are:

- Active listening
- Questionnaires
- Observation
- Checklists
- Formal interviews.

Active listening: Seek out members of the target group or those who work with the group and discusses their needs with them. The person who collects data does not manipulate the conversation but rather records all answers and clarifies responses to questions.

Questionnaires: Pose brief yes/no questions to which answers are checked. These questions can request information, gather opinions, or assess attitudes. The questionnaire can be self-administered with simple questions at the beginning or it can be administered in person to members of the target group or those who work with them. Questionnaires mailed to service providers may receive an expected return of about 30 percent, unless followed up with a telephone call.

Observation: Observe the target group at a community site recording what is seen or heard, but do not interact with patrons, staff, or others. For example, one could observe what happens when parents bring children to adult learning centers or library-based programs. The observer will look for certain behaviors and make note of them.

Checklist: Draw up a list of items directly or indirectly related to needs characteristic of the target group (this should be verified by service providers and members of the target group).

Formal or structured interview: Ask specific questions of all respondents. Usually the same number of questions is asked of each individual and the time frame for responding to the questions is the same length to ensure accuracy.

7. PROJECT DESIGN

The project design is made up of *goals, objectives,* and *activities* which will carry your project forward. In federal proposals, this may be called the *Plan of Operation.* A timeline which charts major action steps listing the person responsible for carrying out those activities may be included here. This will provide the blueprint for the project.

Goals and Objectives

The goals and objectives section are the areas which new proposal writers traditionally find most difficult because the ultimate outcome or long-range goal is frequently confused with the concrete, specific, or short-term outcome for a proposed project.

Goals serve as guiding statements of purpose. They are broad and describe a state of being (for the target group) which may be ideal. In any case, they describe a condition for the long run. Goals may not, and probably will not, be accomplished by the end of the project year. The goal relates directly back to the statement of need.

Sample Goals for a Literacy Project

1. Using the multi-pronged approach of a trained volunteer tutor corps in concert with computer-assisted tools, the library-led collaborative will improve the literacy level of area adults whose skills are currently not sufficient to fulfill their own self-determined objectives.
2. To improve employment prospects for linguistic minorities by providing space, materials, and equipment for ESL/literacy classes with a focus on job search strategies.

In the first example, the target group is named (area adults whose skills are currently not sufficient)—the aim will be to improve their level of literacy. In the second example, the target group is linguistic minorities—the long run condition will be their improved employment prospects resulting from participating in English as a Second Language (ESL) classes. Note that these goals are very broad. They do not state specific numbers of people to be served. There is no time factor or measureable goals to show achievement or success.

Objectives

Objectives are the outcomes of the project and should not be confused with goals (broad, ideal, long-range and maybe difficult to attain) or action steps. The difference between goals and objectives is the difference between intention and interim achievement. Goals are broad in scope and objectives are more specific. The difference between action steps, activities, and objectives is means (activities) and ends (objectives).

Objectives are the concrete, specific, measurable, outcomes/outputs for your project. They specify the ends and achieve your expectations. They state what you plan to accomplish in your program/project. Although they include identifiable activities, they are more elaborate.

When you write an objective you will state:

- Who the target group and staff are.
- What action you will take.
- How many pepole are involved.
- When the program will take place.
- Under what conditions it will take place.
- How the process will be documented for evaluation.

Sometimes these objectives are measured by observation or inspection. Either you have developed fifteen family literacy kits or you haven't. If you intend to set up a special family learning center by the end of the project year, you can prove if this has been accomplished.

Some objectives are measured by quantity such as output measures (e.g. the number of books circulated to adult learners), the number of requests for literacy tutoring, and the number of tutors trained and matched with adult learners. They are a measure of service provided by the project.

Other examples of measurable criteria may include:

1. Time units (within three months, by the end of the project year).
2. Number aggregates (a total of 250 adult new reader materials will be placed in the adult learning center library).

If each objective is expressed as a *single* outcome/output, at the end of the funding year, the project director should be able to answer the question, "To what degree did we accomplish what we set out to do?"

On the other hand, although most libraries and small agencies do not write complicated research proposals with specific behavioral objectives, there is value in including some objectives which show a positive response from the target group.

Objectives can be written which include a measure of "goodness or effectiveness." For example, 75 percent of participants attending a family workshop will rate them "useful or very useful," "helpful," "informative," and so on, or 90 percent of parents in the family program will read to their child at least twice a week. The impact of a project on changing behavior within the target group is hard to measure, especially within a twelve month time frame. It will be examined more closely under the section on evaluation.

Look at the following two examples from a library proposal:

Sample Objectives

Objective 1: Within one year, we hope to establish two computer workstations with appropriate software in the library's family learning center. At least 75 learners will utilize this program as measured by the program director's statistics."

Breaking down the objectives you can identify:

Who?	Adult learners.
What the target group will do?	Utilize appropriate software.
By when?	By the end of the project year.
Measurability? (Output)	At least 75 will participate.

In this objective, the "givens" are the establishment of two computer workstations.

Objective 2: "By the end of the project year, we hope to conduct five workshops on topics related to parenting skills. Program participants will attend at least three of these workshops rating them "useful" or "very useful" on a simple survey instruments

Who?	Program participants, e.g. adult learners.
What will target group do?	Attend parenting workshops.
By when?	The end of the project year.
Measurability? (Outcome)	Attendance at three programs and survey response data.

One needs to decide what type of objectives best serve the proposal. Generally, there are two types:

1. *Process or management* (usually carried out by library/agency):

"By the fourth month, we will establish a family learning center within the library which will house a collection of at least 200 print and non-print family reading materials. Circulation statistics will document that each new item circulates at least once by the end of the project year."

(In this example, it is understood that the target group will check out these materials.)

This kind of objective shows a response from the target group, but it does not show the impact of these materials on the group or how their lives may have changed as a result.

2. *The product or performance objective.* This objective will show evidence of some response from the target group, and affect upon them.

For example:

"By the end of the project year, 70 percent of program participants will read regularly to their children at home as measured by a survey instrument and tutor/learner communications."

In this case, you can actually show a response on the part of the target group. In other words, you can answer the question how have the lives of these people been changed by your project. If the project director has collected baseline data on the behaviors of the target population before the project begins, then these behaviors can be compared with post-project levels.

After writing your objectives, review each by asking if they answer the following questions:

1. Does each objective relate to the goal or a step toward that goal?
2. Does it describe the ends (outcome/output), not the means to the end?
3. Does it specify one single accomplishment?
4. Is it measurable? How will you show it has been achieved?
5. Does it include a date or time frame?

Action Plan

The activities in a project proposal demonstrate how the goals and objectives will be carried out. Ordinarily, the categories which may need description as activities are the following:

Obtaining input: Information will be gathered from members of the collaboration and those who work with the target population. This may include conducting interviews with community agencies or members of the target group.

Staffing: This includes both staff who need to be hired or designated to work on the project. Include the duties of posting, advertising, and hiring a person.

Training: What training is necessary for project staff, members of the collaboration, or others connected with the project? This may include training of volunteers. This may also require contracting with outside trainers.

Selection of material and equipment: What family literacy materials including material on parenting, books for low level readers, children's materials, computer-equipment, software, or tape cassette recorders need to be ordered?

Facilities: What arrangements need to be made to set up a discrete area either within a library or community-center to act as a family learning center? This may include plans for some minor renovation or setting up an area with rugs and bookcases.

Programming: Family literacy includes a great deal of programming for adults and children. It may include designing workshops on parenting or reading to children in addition to adult literacy training. Children's programming may include childhood activities and some joint parent-child events.

Publicity: To recruit parents to participate in the family program is critical. Project staff may need to disseminate program information through local media (radio and cable television). The program may choose to develop brochures written in simple English (or a second language) to publicize the program.

The action plan/project activities should describe how the project will unfold. The number of programs and persons to be reached will be detailed in the objectives but a monthly timeline of action steps will explain when these events will take place. If the starting and ending months are not known, number the months from one to twelve.

Detail how your project will proceed, specifying what will be achieved and by when. The inclusion of a timeline provides a checklist for the project director and keeps the program on target.

The Project Rationale

As part of the project design, a *project rationale* statement presents the reasons why you have chosen your proposed solution. It provides an opportunity to discuss alternative solutions or ideas which may have been considered but were later discarded. A discussion in this area often answers questions which may arise in the mind of the proposal reader about why a specific approach was chosen.

8. BUDGET AND NARRATIVE:

The budget section explains project costs and justifies the amount of money being requested. Most proposal sections include the following standard categories:

- Personnel
- Teaching materials (books, library materials, computer software)
- Equipment
- Supplies
- Travel
- Contractual costs
- Indirect costs and overhead
- Other (printing, advertising)

The budget section provides a detailed breakdown of project-related costs. The total amount of funds requested should be realistic and based on how much money is actually needed to carry out the project. Two parallel columns should list those funds requested from the funder (grant funds or LSCA Title VI) and those funds which will represent a local contribution or in some cases a matching amount. Sometimes an "in-kind" expense which would be local time/resources spent on the project is acceptable and will be described by the funder. Do not inflate your costs. Seasoned proposal readers are astute at picking up padded budgets. Do your homework and verify all project costs.

All requests should relate directly to the project objectives. Any equipment requests should be carefully detailed in the project design. There should be no surprises in the budget section. For example, the proposal reader should not suddenly encounter a request for three computers in the budget section without a clear description of how this equipment fits within the project design.

Most standard proposal applications will provide a detailed explanation of how to list and justify costs. For example, the LSCA Title VI *Budget Information* section from the most recent Application for Grants gives careful explanation on how to report specific budget items.

The following notes may be helpful on categories which are literacy proposals.

Personnel: Include only salary and wages here for those who will be paid specifically from the grant for project-related work. Indicate the number of hours per week each person will work and list their hourly rate. Benefits such as insurance or retirement may be included in this section or in a separate, fringe benefits section.

Travel: Under federal LSCA Title VI guidelines, this section is used only to report the non-local travel of project employees. For example, if the project director needed to travel out-of-state to visit a family literacy site it would justifiably be listed here. In some foundation proposals, local travel costs might be listed as well. In all cases, transportation costs for project staff, consultants, and program participants should be quoted at the local rate.

Equipment: Under LSCA Title VI guidelines, this section includes all expendable property with a value of *more* than $5,000 per unit. For other funders, this may be the section to list all equipment requests. In all cases, equipment requests should include the cost per unit and if possible, a source. Be sure to consult an AV vendor to get the best cost estimate.

Supplies: Under LSCA Title VI guidelines, this section includes all expendable property with a value of *less* than $5,000 per unit. In other proposals, this category may be the place to list tutor workbooks, pencils, special book bags with a project logo, or any item which will need to be replaced from time to time.

Contractual Services: These services require a secondary contract for persons/organizations that are not on the agency or library payroll. You should indicate if the figures are estimated or based on a negotiated amount. If the person performing the contractual service is known, (e.g. an employee of Literacy Volunteers of America) you may want to include a resume and job description of the service in the appendix of the proposal.

Other: This is the "catch-all" category under the LSCA Title VI guidelines. Some of the most common costs listed here are telephone, publicity, miscellaneous travel costs, and honoraria for program speakers. Any state or local municipality such as a public library, city funded adult learning center, or local school should be advised that if their community receives more than $25,000 in federal funds (from all combined sources) they must conduct an audit in accordance with the Education Department General Administration Regulations (EDGAR) for federal grants as published in the Catalog of Federal Regulations (July 1990). It would be wise to consult the guidelines for federal funding to see if an audit would be required and to budget accordingly.

9. AGENCY CAPABILITIES

Many proposals request an explanation of space and equipment availability to manage a project. This topic relates to the *Needs Statement* and *Project Rationale* previously covered and may reiterate the same points. In this section one must establish the identity of the organization/library. When completing LSCA Title VI projects, it is not uncommon to attach a standard form which details statistics on library budget, hours open, number of volumes owned, population served, etc. This background information establishes the credibility of the organization and strengthens the proposal.

10. EVALUATION

The evaluation section will demonstrate how you will document the success of the project objectives. It will detail the strengths and weaknesses of the project in meeting the needs of the target group.

Two Types of Evaluation

There are two types of evaluation which will measure project outcomes and outputs. Sometimes called by different names, they serve two distinct purposes: Ongoing, process, or *formative* evaluation, and final, product or *summative* evaluation. Both types are useful in providing an effective project evaluation.

The formative evaluation allows the project staff to revise any ongoing strategies during the course of the grant year allowing for mid-course corrections as needed. The summative evaluation will enable staff to decide at the end of the project's term if they will continue the project as designed, modify it, or discontinue it.

The evaluation will answer the question, were you able to accomplish what you set out to do? It will tell you:

1. If the desired outcomes/outputs were attained.
2. If the timetable was realistic.
3. The strengths and weaknesses of the complete project.

Four Steps to Evaluation

There are four steps to the evaluation process:

- Evaluation design
- Data collection
- Interpretation of information
- Application.

1. The *Evaluation Design* will answer the following questions:

- What information is useful to inform decision making?
- How can this information be obtained?
- Who will collect this information?
- When will the information be collected?

Debra Wilcox Johnson, in her training component for the ALA-Bell Atlantic Family Literacy project, suggests some important behavioral changes to look for as a result of participation in a family literacy project. Among the factors are: changes in reading habits, attendance by families at library or family center programs, participation in parenting workshops, and an increase in the retention rates in literacy programs. A fuller discussion of evaluation is contained in *Evaluating Library Literacy Programs: A Manual for Reporting Accomplishments,* developed by Debra Wilcox Johnson for the New York State Library.

2. In the *Data Collection* stage you will decide what tools can be used to collect the information. Each evaluation instrument will:

- Use a valid measurement
- Measure each objective reliably

By gathering information about the target population at the beginning of the project year, you collect baseline data for comparison with results which will be accomplished at the end of the project. This is the proof that the program has attained its objectives.

Among the data collection tools which may be used are:

- Interviews with members of the target group.
- Group interviews (including focus groups).
- Journal records or observations of programs.
- Questionnaires and surveys.
- Records of changes brought about through project implementation.
- For library projects, circulation of adult literacy materials, circulation of children's books/family kits; registration of library cards; attendance at family literacy events.
- Comparison with current or pre-project levels of services.
- Pre- and post-assessment of adult learners/children using both standardized and modified instruments.
- Portfolio assessment of work samples developed by parents and children.

3. In the *Summary* step of the evaluation process, all the information collected should be summarized and interpreted. This section will answer the question how do you know you did what you set out to do?

A post-project assessment (using the same instruments from the pre-project phase) may be conducted at the conclusion of the project. This may demonstrate that: a) the conditions of need have continued to increase *despite* the implementation of the project, or b) that although conditions may still be unfavorable, other or unexpected results have taken place as a result of the project.

4. The *Application* step requires application of data collected through the evaluation process. The answers will inform you as to what you will do next. Changes in the program schedule should be based on what you have learned. You may choose to expand, modify, or discontinue the program as a result of these findings. Funders usually require quarterly or final reports to show the results of a project. This Handbook, for instance, is an outgrowth of an evaluation of the Massachusetts CCFL project.

11. KEY PERSONNEL

In this section, you will include all project personnel who have a significant responsibility for the project. The project director should be listed along with a job description and some explanation about specific project responsibilities and the amount of time it will take to manage this program. Any project staff who will be paid out of the proposal should be listed. If you have already identified personnel to be hired (e.g. a child care specialist or an adult literacy teacher) then you should include a job description of their duties and copies of their resumes in the appendix of the proposal.

12. COOPERATION/COLLABORATION

Key players who make up a community collaboration or state/corporate leaders, as discussed in the section "Key Elements of Community Collaboration," may be the most important supporters included in this section of the proposal.

You may choose to list each agency/organization and the name of the staff person who is a member of your community team. If one agency, such as the public library or adult learning center submits the proposal and acts as fiscal agent on behalf of the collaboration, other members of the collaborative team should write a letter of support on agency letterhead. If requested, letters should be included in the appendix of the proposal. It would be helpful if each letter detailed specific support provided by the cooperating agency, such as program space, photocopying privileges, or staff time which will be devoted to the project. Proposal readers may carefully review any letter of support, therefore encourage your supporters to be as specific and detailed as possible about the success of your proposal and its impact on their constituents. In the introduction to this section, you may want to give a brief history of the development of your community collaboration if this is not included in another part of the proposal. A broad range of support letters, from public, private, municipal, regional, and even state level support, demonstrates that you have spent a great deal of time planning this project.

13. APPENDIXES

Among the documents which can be included if required are:

- Letters of support.
- Resumes.
- Job descriptions.
- A map of the community.
- Copies of any questionnaires which were administered to the target population as part of the assessment.
- Evaluation instruments (such as a simple post-project survey).
- Any relevant program brochure which may document your literacy program.
- Copies of any material produced by your project such as a booklet of adult new reader stories or project newsletter.
- Newspaper clippings which support the need or refer to the services provided by your agency.

6
FUNDING AND TECHNICAL ASSISTANCE FOR FAMILY LITERACY

All state libraries in the United States are designated to administer federal monies under the Library Services and Construction Act (LSCA) Title I. Many states run a competitive program which includes a breadth of special services to second-language speakers, children, the elderly, and the disabled with information and referral and literacy services for which only public and institution libraries may apply. Each state sets its own guidelines for funding. Those interested in information about timetable and schedules should make contact with the Head of Library Development, Grants Manager, or equivalent position at the state library agency in their own state.

Priorities are set each year in the event that the request for funds exceeds the total amount of available federal funds. In all cases, LSCA funds are considered "seed money" to begin new programs and services. They require a commitment of future local funds, however, to ensure continuation of the project beyond the funding year.

Grants

LSCA TITLE VI:
THE LIBRARY LITERACY PROGRAM

The Office of Educational Research and Improvement (OERI) of the U.S. Department of Education administers a discretionary grant program—LSCA Title VI, the Library Literacy program. Now in its seventh year, the annual LSCA Title VI budget is close to 8 million dollars per year with a ceiling amount of $35,000 per project. In recent years, the number of family literacy programs funded under LSCA Title VI has increased steadily perhaps in recognition of the excitement generated by a new approach to literacy which reinforces the historical role of the library as a center for lifelong learning for families. As the success of other library-based family programs continues to be publicized, Title VI has became an increasingly important source for programs which require the critical second or third year funding necessary to establish a program within a community. Under the most recent guidelines for this program, the word "adult" was inserted to emphasize that the Library Literacy Program specifically targets adults. Family literacy projects will be funded but the emphasis of teaching should be on the adult. This program will not support activities that focus on improving the skills of children. A project which is written in collaboration with other agencies can use support monies from local or other sources to provide support activities for children such as story hours, family events, and children's books. This highly competitive program is administered directly from Washington and requires a well constructed proposal which demonstrates a strong degree of cooperation and collaboration. The funding cycle runs from October to September with proposals submitted by late Fall of the previous year.

BARBARA BUSH FOUNDATION FOR FAMILY LITERACY

The Barbara Bush Foundation for Family Literacy was established in March, 1989 and provides a small number of demonstration grants for family literacy. Although the total number of funded programs is small, those agencies fortunate enough to receive funding have enjoyed a great deal of prestige. In the first year only eleven programs were funded nationwide with another thirteen projects selected this past fall. In view of the highly competitive nature of the program, it was a tribute to the high quality of the project design that the only library-based family literacy program in the nation awarded in the first year went to the Lawrence (MA) Public Library's *Newcomers Family Literacy Program*.

NATIONAL CENTER FOR FAMILY LITERACY

The National Center for Family Literacy (NCFL) in Louisville, Kentucky is a private, non-profit corporation the mission of which is to develop and expand the concept of family literacy nationwide. The Center is supported from a generous grant from the William R. Kenan, Jr. Charitable Trust. The Center provides training and dissemination of a program model called *Kenan Trust Family Literacy Project*. The center promotes public awareness through information seminars, and implementation of the family literacy project model. This model provides adult education instruction to parents and early childhood education to the children of adult learners. The program currently has adaptations of the Kenan Trust model in 62 sites in 27 states. An estimated 1,300 families participated in this program in 1990.

This past year, the Toyota Motor Corporation provided funds to the National Center for Family Literacy to implement a *Toyota Families for Learning Program* that will utilize the Kenan Trust model. The communities that received funding to implement the Toyota program are all working to build community partnerships among education, libraries, and social service agencies.

THE EVEN START FAMILY LITERACY PROGRAM

Perhaps the greatest impact for the development and support of family literacy initiatives is the expansion of funds under Even Start to include more funding for family literacy programs. The Even Start Program, which now enters its fifth year, was originally a federal program that provided funding for demonstration projects through the United States Department of Education to approximately 150 school districts across the country. Under the National Literacy Act, the program has now been designated the *Even Start Family Literacy Program* and in July of 1992, became a state administered program under the Elementary and Secondary Education Act of 1965. It allows states to make a minimum grant of $75,000 for each program and targets services to both parents and their children from birth to age eight.

Know Your Funding Guidelines

Here is an example of criteria to be addressed in the *Application For Grants Under The Library Literacy Program* or the Library Services and Construction Act (LSCA) Title VI proposal. The elements and order required in a final proposal are outlined in most application packages. In the LSCA Title VI application, the criteria for funding is published in the Federal Register and a copy is included in the application. However, federal proposal applications can seem extremely daunting to the first-time writer.

Other funding agencies may use a totally different format and request a presentation of the finished proposal with similar elements but in a different order. A score or a number of points is allocated to each element. Usually the total score is 100 points. LSCA Title VI proposals should be structured section by section as suggested in the criteria section of the application packet. A proposal reviewer will respond to a sheet which lists the criteria and allocates a certain number of points for each category. If sections are missing, the reviewer will deduct points. In a competitive federal grant round such as LSCA Title VI or the National Institute for Literacy, two or three points may well make the difference between being funded or not. The federal government requires that agencies demonstrate how they will meet affirmative action and civil rights guidelines in the proposal. For example, in the Title VI proposal, there are several areas where one must actually state how the project will be made equally accessible. Do not assume that the grant reader will be able to extract an affirmative action statement or policy from a generalized statement in the proposal. Rather, it is better to spell it out.

The following points are based on the LSCA Title VI criteria for funding found in the most recent Catalog of Federal Domestic Assistance (CFDA). These criteria which are contained in the proposal application are annotated with some extra comments provided for those who may find the criteria difficult to interpret.

CRITERIA FOR TITLE VI PROPOSALS

Need
(25 points)
- Show the extent of concentration of adults who do not have a secondary education or its equivalent in the area served by the project.
- Explain whether the community or financial resources are available without federal assistance.
- Include the per capita income and rate of unemployment in the area served by the project.

Additional suggestions . . .
- In order to earn points, the applicants must show that target adults meet the criteria of unemployment or underemployment.

Coordination
(25 points)
- Identify providers of literacy-related services, including state or local adult education agencies or community-based organizations.
- Identify the services provided by these parties.
- Demonstrate communication with officials or their representatives.
- Indicate specific measures for cooperation and coordination.

Additional suggestions . . .
- List specific outside supporters by agency and indicate the capacity in which each agency will work with the library (e.g. as an advisory board member). Refer to the support letter from that agency person (include this letter in the attachment section). Specifically state what the role of other literacy organizations will be in providing publicity, support services, training, etc.

Plan of Operation
(20 points)
- Develop a project design of high quality.
- Clearly describe how the project objectives relate to the needs of the population.
- Include specific outcomes (e.g. measurable objectives).

- Show how objectives can be evaluated.
- Design a project which will take place within the project year (12 months).
- Include an effective plan of management (action plan).
- Show how personnel and resources can be used to achieve each objective.
- Include a distinct role for state or local libraries.
- Include an efficient timeline for meeting each objective.
- Include a clear description of how the applicant will provide equal access and treatment for members of racial or ethnic minorities, women, disabled, and the elderly.

Additional suggestions . . .

- State the objectives as the desired outcomes which will happen as a result of this project.
- Describe your plans for implementing this project in chronological order.
- Consider what resources are necessary and include them in the action plan.
- Consider any special training or publicity that will be necessary to accomplish your objectives.

Quality of Key Personnel
(15 points)

- The qualifications of the project director (should include a resume).
- The qualifications of other key personnel (include resume and/or job descriptions).
- Indicate the time that project director/others will spend on the project (be realistic).
- The extent to which the applicant, as part of its nondiscriminatory employment practices, encourages applications for employment from members of racial or ethnic minorities, women, disabled, and the elderly.

Additional suggestions . . .

- Demonstrate experience and training in the fields related to the objectives.
- Duties of the project director should include responsibility for project management and reporting.
- Be specific about the actual project-related work key personnel will perform.
- Mention specific staff members or personnel having experience with target group.

Budget and Cost Effectiveness
(10 points)

- Make sure this is a cost effective project (don't pad budget).
- Show how the budget is adequate to support the activities.
- Make sure costs are reasonable in relationship to objectives.

Additional suggestions . . .

- Be sure all items relate directly to objectives and activities.
- Explain any unusual items or amounts.
- Break down personnel by hours and days worked, including fringe benefits (be explicit).

- Round off request to the nearest dollar.
- Include any local (in-kind) costs which will be contributed to make project services/materials accessible to the target group.

Evaluation
(15 points)
- The extent to which the methods of evaluation are appropriate and objective, producing data which is measurable and quantifiable.
- Determine how successful the project is in meeting its intended outcomes.

Additional suggestions . . .
- Specify the kinds of data to be collected and maintained.
- Show how each objective will be measured.
- Include measures of usage for comparison to pre-project levels.
- Use an advisory committee to conduct periodic evaluations of progress as well as a final evaluation.
- Use both formative (ongoing) and summative (final) evaluation measures.

Adequacy of Resources
(5 points)
- Demonstrate the extent to which the facilities are adequate.
- Explain why the equipment and supplies the applicant plans to use are adequate.

Additional suggestions . . .
- Describe the community, the library, and the services provided to the target group.
- Describe why the library/support agencies are capable of managing these projects.
- Explain the library's previous experience with the target group.
- Include specific physical requirements—space, equipment, and supplies—necessary to implement this project and show how they will strengthen the project.

Tips for Proposal Writers

1. After you have finished all the work on the proposal, go back and read it over carefully and check for grammar, spelling, and punctuation. Include an outline as an aid to the reviewer.
2. Share your proposal with someone outside of your profession who can check if it is written in understandable English. The best proposals are clear, concise, and free of jargon.
3. Don't inflate your in-kind contribution and be sure your budget adds up. Use a calculator.
4. Don't make unsupported claims or assume that the reviewer knows about your organization. If it is relevant to the proposal put it in!

5. Address all questions in the application or in the criteria. Leaving something out, such as your community's unemployment figures, may cost you points and the final grant.
6. Write as much as you are requested to. Do not exceed the number of pages requested.
7. Double check that original signatures are on all documents and that any required attachments such as assurances are included. If outside agency signatures are needed, such as a town manager or government official, do not wait until the last minute to get your proposal signed.
8. Double check your deadlines. Given the competition for funding, a proposal submitted after the due date will not be considered.

Sometimes, in spite of all your planning and hard work the proposal is not funded the very first time. This may be in part due to the competitive nature of the grant round. However, most funding agencies will supply you with some written comments which can help you rewrite the proposal for future funding cycles. Pay careful attention to the criteria in the application instructions and strictly adhere to any written guidelines. If you are successful and your proposal is selected for funding, carefully collect the necessary data to evaluate your project. This will provide valuable documentation for subsequent requests for new or expanded projects.

Final Thoughts:

A history of working with grants has proved the following axioms to be true:

1. Everything takes more time than you originally thought it would.
2. Equipment, materials, or any other tangible items you may wish to order will be delayed, out of stock, or cost more than you originally budgeted.
3. The staff which you planned to hire or were counting on will leave town, go on maternity leave, or not do the job which you thought they could do.

Be prepared to be creative and flexible.
People from agencies and organizations who embark upon collaborative relationships may frequently find they are moving two steps forward and one step backwards in an effort to come up with new solutions to old problems. Collaboration is hard work and, like proposal writing, is best learned by doing.

Many family literacy success stories are recounted in both print and video resources listed at the end of this Handbook. They should serve as inspiration to potential proposal writers. Members of a collaboration must tailor their programs to fit precisely with the needs of their individual communities. The strong emphasis on cooperative planning presented here must be combined with the intangible factors, the dedication and commitment, of the team members. With these two factors present, community collaboratives may advance the concept of family literacy beyond design into the reality of a fully functional program. Visualize a program with the potential to change the lives of adult learners and their children beyond anything imagined by the group when those tentative, uncertain meetings first took place.

APPENDIX A

THE MASSACHUSETTS COMMUNITY COLLABORATION FOR FAMILY LITERACY PROJECT MODEL

Background and Need in Massachusetts

Massachusetts, like our nation, is facing a great crisis. While our government wrestles with an agenda of budget cuts, the "shelf life" of our disadvantaged children and their at-risk families is expiring.

The national picture is mirrored in Massachusetts where parents living at or below the poverty level are five times more likely to be functionally illiterate than those with a yearly income of $15,000 or more.

In Massachusetts:

- 1.4 million people, or one in five adults, lack a high school diploma.
- At least 30 percent of the Hispanic population is living below the poverty level with a 13.8 percent unemployment rate.
- 40 percent of the average urban high school population made up predominantly of minorities drops out before graduation.

Moreover, nearly one-half million children live in families where at least one parent has insufficient skills to read aloud with the child, help him with homework or be an advocate for the child at school.

Working parents, including a growing number who are single women, have less time to spend with their children. Since 1970, the number of female heads of household has increased by 97 percent, with one in three living in poverty. Many of these women are teenagers who lack the basic skills to make informed decisions about child rearing and parenting.

Research has shown that the greatest predictor of a child's success in school is the literacy level of the parent, especially the mother.

The Massachusetts Office for Children reports that about two- thirds of working mothers maintain their preschool children in some kind of child care facility and that 33,000 school-age children are enrolled in extended day programs. However, many of those not in afterschool care show up as library latchkey children who wait unsupervised in local libraries. There they become an added responsibility for staff who want to see them constructively occupied.

Under the current Massachusetts Long Range Plan for Library Development 1991-96, the MBLC targeted family literacy and the development of library family learning centers as a top funding priority. Given this authority, the agency's literacy consultant wrote and received funding under the Library Services and Construction Act (LSCA Title VI) for a proposal which was designed to enable local public libraries to serve the literacy needs of at-risk families. It provided coordination of a state- wide planning model, Community Collaborations for Family Literacy (CCFL) to develop family literacy projects in local communities.

The CCFL project was developed in response to an identified need within the Massachusetts library community. In spite of a fair amount of interagency cooperation at the state level, there was an observable lack of coordination at the local level where family literacy programs must be implemented. A variety of agencies across the Commonwealth continue to address different areas of family needs. Libraries are not often tied into the network of other community agencies which share the common goal of providing services to families.

While forty-two libraries are currently involved in active literacy programs, many other libraries continue to be under-utilized resources for serving the needs of adult learners and families "at risk."

The barriers to greater library participation are sometimes related to turf issues, (e.g. which agency/organization is taking the lead role in providing basic literacy services in the community). Libraries frequently lack the public relations skills to promote the wealth of services they could provide in support of local literacy and social service programs. Moreover, they are often subject to an institutional inertia. They are frequently mired in a concept of service which is best able to serve only those who walk through their doors or they are too overwhelmed just trying to keep those doors open. There are still many who believe it is not the library's mandate to be involved in literacy services or that the real solution to the problem is to simply ensure that every child has a library card. While every child should have and use a library card, ownership of the library card alone will not guarantee a child's success if the parent is unable to support and foster those all-important literacy activities at home.

In the second year of funding, local educational agencies in the state were invited to submit proposals to develop comprehensive strategies for family literacy under the federal Even Start legislation. Unfortunately, even though community collaboration was identified as a critical part of the planning effort, the majority of proposals were put together with little coordination. In the past three years, only one Massachusetts proposal submitted for Even Start considered developing a role for its local library as part of the overall project design.

In the past few years, a number of libraries in the Commonwealth have implemented projects which are "family or intergenerational" in nature. They provide story hours, lapsits, and read aloud sessions for at-risk groups. They purchased expanded quantities of paperbacks, board books, and early childhood materials. They developed specialized parenting collections and gave workshops on how to use these collections. Outreach programs to daycare, childcare, and adult learning centers have broadened the concept of the traditional "school visit." Deposit collections and programming in family shelters, afterschool programs for latchkey children, and a program designed for inmate mothers in a local prison have given community library services a new image. No two programs are exactly alike and each was developed by determining the appropriate role for the library as part of a strategy to better coordinate services with other local providers in their own community.

For example, Massachusetts libraries in Quincy, Lawrence, and Springfield expanded their outreach efforts to develop a new library support role for family literacy. Programs were begun which coordinated basic skills instruction to adults with complementary reading and literacy activities for their children. These library-based projects were among the first in the state to respond to a critical need for greater library collaboration with adult and children's literacy experts. The libraries provided training for staff about issues related to the cultural differences of newly literate or at-risk families. As successful programs, they nevertheless represented a limited number. There was an evident need to expand this kind of family literacy model to other Massachusetts communities.

As Ruth Nickse writes so forcefully in the *Noises of Literacy*, "It is not easy to reshape the image of the library as an egalitarian community resource that serves many populations—including low literate children and the poor. It entails a new vision of local library services and credit must go to those who make this vision operational, especially in a time of scarce resources. Library programs should continue to expand, despite these difficulties, since they can be a valuable form of indirect intervention in support of literacy."

THE STATE CONTEXT FOR COMMUNITY COLLABORATIONS

Community Collaborations for Family Literacy was developed in 1990-91 in the midst of a severe financial crises in Massachusetts which affected both the state and local contexts of the project. The economic recession led to massive cutbacks in all human service programs including library services across the state. The election of a conservative Governor promised to reduce the state budget while raising no new taxes, although admirable in intent, created a condition of uncertainty and near chaos in the human service delivery area. This condition is mirrored across the New England states in general. Cities and towns hard pressed to maintain adequate staffing of police and fire departments, education, health care, and programs for the disadvantaged have pitted libraries against these "essential services." As the white collared middle class joins the pink and blue collared in the unemployment lines, manpower and morale in the state have been severely reduced in private and public sector employment alike.

Libraries of course, have faced cutbacks in funding at both the state and local level. Many libraries have seriously reduced hours of operation, laid off staff, closed branch services, and drastically cut book budgets in an effort to deal with diminishing local aid.

These circumstances restricted the choice of participant communities to those with enough staff willing to take on a new project in less than ideal circumstances. At on-site visits, the plight of each individual community was expressed in vivid detail. Library staff members related the frustration of a dramatic increase in use of the library facility by the formerly employed at a time when cuts in library staff resulted in less than adequate services. This is the context in which the Community Collaborations for Family Literacy was created, and against which its successes and failures are measured.

In the participating local communities, already overburdened staff were remarkable in the intensity with which they supported the CCFL project and in the amount of time and effort they devoted to networking and building local teams. Indeed, the very hardships each community faced seemed to act as a force for uniting around a common purpose—how to better serve low literate adults and children with increasingly limited resources.

The Community Collaborations for Family Literacy Project was designed in recognition of the fact that developing services to reach both adults and children requires long term and careful planning and coordination. Too frequently, when the concept of family literacy captures the imagination of an individual in a library, adult learning center, or family support agency, the first reaction is to seek funding to put a program in place without laying the critical foundation of cooperative planning.

Massachusetts has maintained a working group of state agency providers which provide funding for literacy services designated as the *Governor's Interagency Literacy Group* (ILG). Representatives of the ILG met over the past four years to coordinate guidelines for basic skills. They developed a common language and guidelines for clients who responded to a State Request for Proposals (RFP) in order to most effectively sustain existing programs and provide funding for new initiatives.

In the past three years, two library-based programs have received support heretofore unavailable through the Massachusetts Department of Education. Moreover, library-based literacy programs continue to receive funding through the Commonwealth Literacy Campaign which is under the direction of the Massachusetts Department of Education.

Adult education, social service providers, and librarians involved in community outreach share the common characteristic of being stretched in too many different directions. All too frequently, when a source of funds is announced, an agency or library will hastily put together a proposal in response to a Request for Proposals (RFP). Overburdened staff are under time constraints which prevent them from conducting a thorough examination of community needs. At certain times of the year, there is a flurry of frantic proposal writing during which community providers are asked for support letters from another agency. Supporters frequently write these letters at the last minute and with no real understanding of the project they are endorsing. It is no small wonder that five or seven months later, when funding becomes available, agencies need to be reminded that they have committed themselves and sometimes their staff to a project about which they know little or nothing.

The CCFL project was designed to change that relationship. It was developed in recognition of the fact that to be truly effective in reaching out to at-risk families all community agencies must be involved at all levels in the design, development, and implementation of a project. The design of family literacy programs must be based on a realistic understanding of the needs of the target group and the development must reflect a shared vision among all community agencies on how to best meet those needs.

THE COMMUNITY COLLABORATIONS FOR FAMILY LITERACY PROJECT DESIGN

The Community Collaborations for Family Literacy project was designed to improve the ability of libraries in Massachusetts to:

- Enhance existing library literacy programs through the addition of a family component.
- Develop library family learning centers especially for working and single parents that focus on literacy, parenting skills, child development, and career skills.
- Increase the use of the library by at risk adult learners and their families through programming and special collections.
- Develop partnerships among community agencies serving a shared population.

Project Methodology

The timeline of this project stretched from October, 1990 to January 1992. However, as with all projects, there was a tremendous amount of pre-planning which went on before the project started and post-project evaluation and assessment which followed. In the summer of 1990, the project director met with the Educational consultant, Dr. Nickse, and some members of the Governor's Interagency Literacy Group to discuss which Massachusetts communities would be best able to participate in this project. We wanted to establish collaborative programs across a broad geographic area of the state reflecting the variety of settings—focusing on urban, suburban, and rural communities around the state.

In the case of all but one site, there was no existing adult literacy program actually taking place within the library. The concept of this project as outlined by the project director was to involve the library in the development of a plan for family literacy. It was not intended to establish an adult literacy program in the library. Rather, the approach was to raise awareness about the issue of family literacy within the library and allow each community to best design a program which would meet their own unique needs.

After initial consultation, seven possible project sites were selected and an invitational letter was sent to the director of each library. In several cases, the project director also made contact with the local adult education provider in each community to ascertain possible interest in participating in this project.

PARTICIPANT COMMITMENT

The letter requested the following commitments from each library:

- As the lead agency, the library would identify a committed, resourceful staff person to work as the principal contact for the community collaborations project.
- The library representative would attend an all-day training session which was held in December, 1990.
- The library staff member would coordinate at least four meetings of a team of community members from January to June 1991 and document these meetings with blank notebooks supplied by the MBLC, flip charts, and an agenda which would reflect the process of team building.
- The project director and educational advisor asked to attend at least one of the four meetings to observe the dynamics of the group process.
- Community team members would attend a Statewide Invitational Conference on Family literacy in June 1991.
- Team members would attend a post session of all community teams in September 1991 to evaluate the project, share their progress in the development of their community plan, and discuss the future of each project.
- In the Fall of 1991, the library would consider submitting a letter of intent requesting LSCA Title I funds for a family literacy project based upon their community plan.

INCENTIVES FOR PARTICIPATION

The incentive for participating in the this planning included:

- Obtaining a new collection of family literacy or family learning materials.
- The opportunity to receive training and to participate in a team building/training with others in their community.
- The opportunity to attend a Family Literacy Conference which would present new ideas and validate emerging theories about what works.

FIGURE A.1. Community Collaborations: Geographic Profiles

COMMUNITY COLLABORATIONS: GEOGRAPHIC PROFILES

Community	Population	Type	Contact	Level of Previous Collaboration	Library	Special Comments	Statewide Location
BROCKTON	92,788	Urban	Linda Braun	Already Established small Family Literacy Collabotative	Brockton Public Library	Municipal Cuts To Library. Collaborative Initiated By Adult Learning Center	South Central
FITCHBURG	41,194	Urban/suburban	Elizabeth Watson	Library/Community Agencies	Fitchburg Public Library	Provided outreach to three communities Sub. Title VI	North Central
GREENFIELD	18,666	Rural	Michael Francheschi	Library/Community Agencies	Greenfield Public Library	Devastated by municipal cuts	West
PEABODY	48,000	Urban/suburban	Mary Ann Tricarico	School/Library	Peabody Institute Library	No adult education participant	North East
SOMERVILLE	76,210	Urban	Ann Dausch	Adult Learning Center	Somerville Public Library	Evenstart Community	Metro Boston
WAREHAM	21,906	Rural	Mary Jane Pillsbury	School/Library Reading Partners	Wareham Public Library	Submitted Title VI Grant Evenstart Community	South East

- The possibility of developing a solid community plan to secure not only LSCA Title I funds but as a basis for other funding.

Technical Assistance and Events

DECEMBER TRAINING WORKSHOP— FRAMINGHAM PUBLIC LIBRARY

The Training Workshop which launched the CCFL project took place in December, 1990 at the Framingham Public Library which is located outside Boston in the Metro West Area of Massachusetts. It was fairly accessible to most of the sites by using the Massachusetts Turnpike and free parking was available for the day. Since this was a statewide project, every effort was made to consider the geographic locations and to build in time for travel. Participants were encouraged to come to the site together. Travel costs were reimbursed through the grant and lunch and refreshments were provided.

Prior to the Framingham Workshop, program participants were given an initial questionnaire requesting information about their participation in the project (see fig. A.6). This was used as a basis for assessing the background and experience of site participants with family literacy and the concept of collaboration.

The agenda was based on a combination of large group discussion, lecture/presentation, and small group discussion with plenty of time for interaction. Team members worked as a group on a community mapping exercises with others many of whom they were not acquainted with. In the course of the day, time was also built in for all librarians, adult basic educators, and school or family service providers to engage in a little "shop talk" with colleagues from other communities. The Framingham Library provided the ideal space for this training. It had an expansive open meeting room where participants initially met in a large circle and later moved chairs around as needed for small group discussion. Participants reported in their final evaluation that overall, the meeting was extremely helpful. However, individual members expressed a wish for more time for small group discussion and the need for more emphasis on how to respond to the specific needs of multicultural populations.

SITE VISITS TO COMMUNITY COLLABORATIONS MEETINGS

The project director visited every community site once and sometimes more often in the course of the project year and the educational consultant observed four collaborative meetings. Another member of the MBLC professional staff also participated in several community site meetings. The purpose of these visits was to:

1. Provide technical assistance and answer questions about the direction of a project or to make suggestions.
2. Observe the dynamics of group collaboration as a process.

In a follow up questionnaire, participants stated that these visits were extremely helpful. As an observer commented, CCFL staff members were available to make suggestions which helped the process to flow a little more smoothly.

In the December training session, the participants were asked to document the group meetings by developing a written agenda for each meeting which would take small steps toward the progress of a final goal. The library participant was asked to document these meetings through written notes and flip charts, and to maintain this information in the CCFL project notebook.

In theory, these meetings had been designed so that the librarian at the community site maintained the notebook of materials and acted as group leader—at least until the community group took shape. In two of six sites, someone other than the librarian ended up assuming responsibility for scheduling the meetings, taking notes, setting the agenda, and serving as the primary contact person with the project director. Nevertheless, there was no perception in the post project interviews with participants that the librarians were less committed to the final outcome of developing a working collaborative. Rather, it seemed that the overwhelming budgetary problems affecting the stressed communities prompted these librarians to delegate the meeting responsibilities to another member of the collaborative.

Almost without exception, the collaborative groups met more than four times in the months before the final letter of intent was due. For example, one community met weekly and another met a total of eight times between January and September, 1991.

As the deadline for the letter of intent drew near, one library decided against filing an application because all branch service had been closed and the main library was open only three days a week. However, the family literacy collaboration was relocated to a school building and the community designated funds to maintain the partnership which currently serves ten families four times a week. The librarian continues to provide support through storytelling for parents and children at the project site.

The Statewide Invitational Conference

BUILDING COMMUNITY COLLABORATIONS FOR FAMILY LITERACY—BENTLEY COLLEGE, WALTHAM, MA.

The statewide invitational family literacy conference, Building Community Collaborations for Family Literacy, took place on June 14, 1991 at Bentley College outside of Boston. It was a key element in the overall success of this project. In addition to bringing together participants from five New England states, it made a vibrant statement about the importance of family literacy to a cross section of leaders in adult education, libraries, early childhood, and school-based programs. It presented a wealth of new ideas, directions and most importantly, an opportunity for participants to pose questions to experts about emergent literacy, the uses of environmental print, cognitive science, and multicultural and intergenerational approaches. It presented family literacy opportunities in settings as diverse as the pediatric clinic and the workplace in addition to the more traditional community and library-based programs. The whole event was video and audio taped in part through the generosity of Bentley College in Waltham. The college runs a Service Learning Project at this predominately business-oriented college and was anxious to more actively involve its students in learning about the needs of the local community.

The family literacy conference demonstrated that collaboration can work not only at the local level, but it can also be effective at the state level. The conference received strong support from the Massachusetts Department of Education, Bureau of Adult Education and was partly sponsored by the state's System for Adult Basic Education (SABES) which provides training and technical assistance to adult education programs statewide. The Dean of Continuing Education at Quinsigamond Community College located in Central Massachusetts generously offered the services of his staff to help with all pre-conference registrations thus relieving the project director of a time consuming but necessary part of conference logistics.

The decision was made to evaluate the impact of the conference several weeks after the event and this proved a valuable approach. Overall, people were more willing to respond to a more detailed questionnaire after they had several weeks to reflect on the ideas generated at the conference. It allowed time for CCFL staff to assess the impact of the conference in terms of actions which had taken place as a result of conference attendance.

As a further indicator of the success of the conference and as a result of providing leadership through the planning and implementation of the CCFL project, the state library continues to receive phone calls and letters requesting

FIGURE A.2.

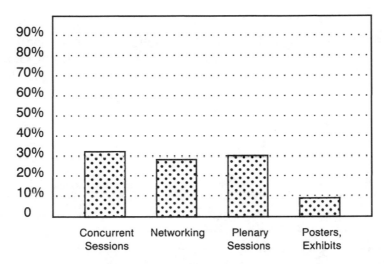

**Building Community Collaborations
For Family Literacy Conference Day**

* Total does not equal 100% due to rounding

1. Concurrent Sessions: (12) = 150 minutes

2. Networking / Registration, 2 coffee hours, lunch, reception: = 140 minutes

3. Plenary Sessions: (3) = 145 minutes

4. Poster Sessions: (3) = 45 minutes

*People were well pleased with the balance between concurrent and plenary
sessions. There was time for networking and time to interact with community
collaboration project directors and to see family literacy materials.*

more information about family literacy and the specific outcomes of the Massachusetts Community Collaborations project plan. The concept of family literacy and the value of a collaborative, cross agency approach seems to make good sense to those struggling to serve families, and people are interested in learning how to begin their own programs.

EVALUATION WORKSHOP

At the end of the project year, and before the letter of intent could be filed with the MBLC for LSCA Title I funds, a half-day meeting with program participants was held at the Shrewsbury Public Library in Central Massachusetts. Participants from four of the six communities attended this meeting, but the collaboration was well represented and included a cross-section of adult educators, librarians, and early childhood/Chapter One providers.

Those present discussed the impact of the project on their individual programs and made suggestions for continuing their collaborative efforts. Information on the funding cycle for both LSCA Titles I and VI was provided.

Program participants generally agreed that the project had an important impact on their thinking. It was especially interesting to note that three adult basic education directors were unanimous in agreeing that they now consistently speak about family literacy as an integral and important part of adult education. One Adult Education Director spoke forcefully on the early success of a pilot family literacy project which had developed as a result of participation in the collaborative when he presented testimony before state legislators this past summer.

PROJECT EVALUATION AND RESULTS

The CCFL project was a first—an experiment in nourishing community planning. The evaluation plan was designed to be descriptive of a year-long process and also to report impacts of the project. It was tailored to record, as much as possible, the ongoing processes of collaborative planning in the six local sites as well as some reasonable outcome measures for the effectiveness of the project. With projects of small size and brief duration and with very limited funding, it seemed advisable to develop an informal, multi-method evaluation plan, which created guidelines that could be used by others.

EVALUATION GOALS

The overall evaluation goals of the project as stated in the proposal included the following:

- Self-evaluation about creating working relationships among the cooperating agencies.

- Collecting information from the six community teams on the process for putting a family literacy planning process in place.
- The effectiveness of the project in promoting community cooperation.
- The extent to which coordination and communication was established between state level interagency efforts and local programs.
- The intent of the participants to maintain their linkages through preparation of plans for a joint family literacy project.
- The extent to which team efforts either succeeded or failed, in their opinions.

The original proposal to the OERI funders did not mention the development of a handbook. However, we wanted a participatory evaluation approach that would involve library staff and community collaborators at each site in data collection that was meaningful and of some use to them and to others in communities that might wish to replicate this project. Thus the concept of the present Handbook developed. Our hope was that the data recorded in the notebooks would give insights into the development of working relationships, as well as the effectiveness of the community cooperation. The in-depth interviews would elaborate on the process, and the presence (or absence) of letters of intent would document the desire to maintain the linkages and act as indicators of success.

At the initial training workshop in December 1990, the idea for a handbook was explained to the participant teams. Each community was given an empty notebook and encouraged to enter agendas, meeting notes, and other memorabilia of the planning process in their communities in the empty notebooks. No particular instructions were given to participants other than that the contents of the notebooks were to be reviewed for insights gained about the collaborative process, in the manner of case studies.

Data Gathering Methods

The evaluation plan included the following measures which were developed by the educational consultant with the project director.

- Site visits by staff.
- Group meetings.
- Two workshops.
- An invitational Conference which prompted informal sharing of information and a barometer of project progress.
- Telephone communications and memos were another means of guiding the project and were used to gather information on processes of collaboration.

SITE MEETING RECORD AND PROCESS
An example of a Site Meeting Record containing pertinent information about meetings was distributed and a process for its use suggest- ed (see fig. A.7). The record was to be kept by the cooperating librarian in each community. With the exception of one community, the project director and the evaluator visited each site separately or together at least once and sometimes more than once during the course of the project year. In addition, a second MBLC educational consultant made site visits and provided technical assistance to communities.

For example, on one of the preliminary site visits, the participants met in a classroom style setting, (e.g. seats facing the person who had convened the meeting). This meeting format somewhat inhibited the full participation of those present and the project staff member attending the meeting suggested that the format be changed to a roundtable or placement of chairs in a circle for future meetings. At another site, it became obvious at the first meeting of more than fifteen representatives, that many agencies had little understanding of the mission or resources of other groups. The two-hour meeting was a pleasant revelation to all present that there were untapped community resources and that new possibilities might be opened up through greater cooperation.

INITIAL QUESTIONNAIRE
A brief questionnaire served as an introduction to the staff about the communities where the projects were sited. The makeup of the participant teams, information about their organizations and their expectations for the project were recorded. This information was filled out and returned at the first joint meeting of all six community teams which was held at the outset of the project.

Results of this questionnaire enabled project staff to gauge the interest of the group. For example, one of the respondents indicated that their facility was currently being underutilized and this project might increase its use by families. Others expressed interest in participating in a project which would provide professional support and stimulation in order to reduce isolation.

Among the barriers which people expressed was a concern that many parents work at odd hours and it might be difficult to design a program which would accommodate them, or a concern that agency staff was already stretched extremely thin and the fear of being able to give sufficient time to a new project.

POST-CONFERENCE QUESTIONNAIRE TO PARTICIPANTS
A post-conference questionnaire was mailed to 260 conference participants to record the perceived benefits of the daylong event, and to attempt to document action steps sparked by the conference itself. While a conference evaluation was included in each attendee's packet, it was considered to be supplemental data. We decided to give the ideas generated at the conference time to settle. Further-

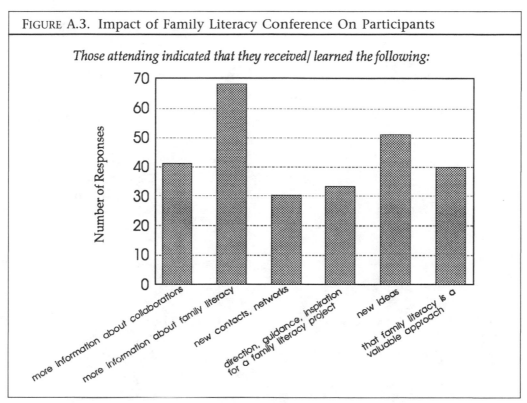

FIGURE A.3. Impact of Family Literacy Conference On Participants

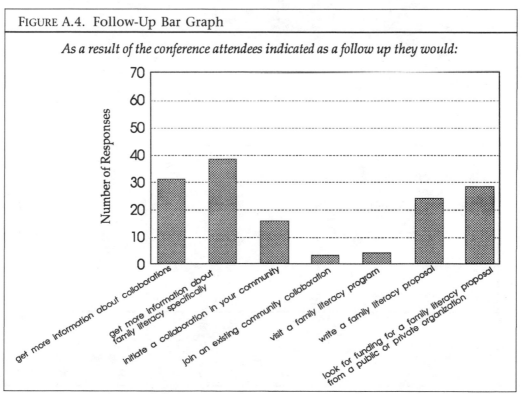

FIGURE A.4. Follow-Up Bar Graph

FIGURE A.5. Resources Necessary—Bar Graph and Number of Respondents

Conference attendees indicated the resources necessary to establish or maintain family literacy were:

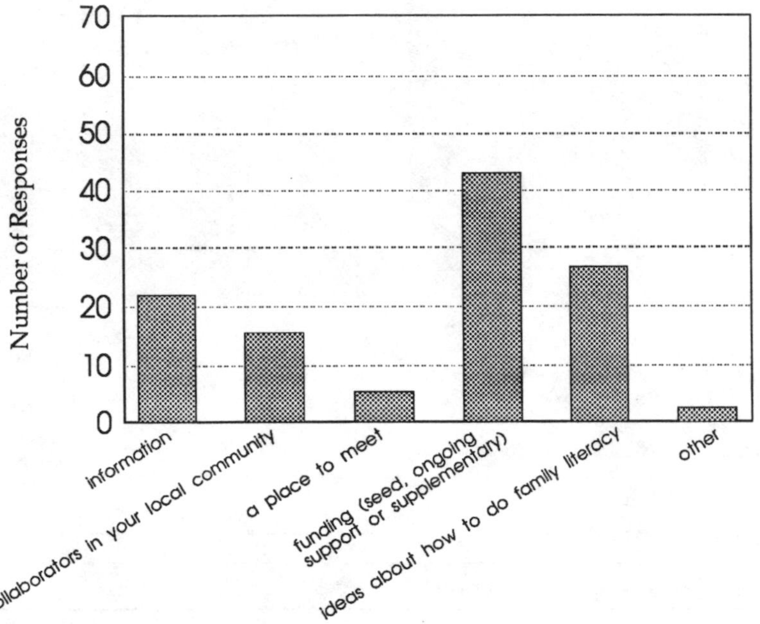

The following number of respondents to the follow-up questionnaire indicated that they would apply for funding from:

Barbara Bush Foundation   6

EVEN START   2

Local/State Agencies   11

Title VI   5

Comments from the Statewide Invitational Conference

"I am thinking of a mini-family literacy project here at work- after hours for employees and kids." (Adult educator at workplace literacy site).

"I enjoyed the conference tremendously! I think it would be helpful to many if it were an annual event held in the fall." (EVEN START Coordinator).

"Our program plans to strengthen the family aspects of our curriculum-helping kids with homework, reading children's books, dealing with schools, family math ... also we'll be trying to include teens with adult learners as mentors this year." (Adult educator in library literacy program).

"EVEN START is always looking to connect with other groups in our community... we have just enlisted RSVP (Retired Seniors Volunteer Program) to help our parents learn to cook and sew." (EVEN START Coordinator).

"I enjoyed the programs very much. I wish that every librarian across the state had attended." (Adult Educator working with library literacy program).

"Volunteers can play a major role in family literacy programs. We are ready and waiting to become involved. What a great day!" (Commonwealth Literacy Campaign director).
"This conference was a great inspiration." (Library literacy coordinator).

"Excellent conference. Filled a tremendous need in Massachusetts. Thank you for all your vision!" (Consultant, Massachusetts Bureau of Adult Education).

"Well organized, focused, diverse presentations. A change for adult literacy, youth and direct care providers from the same agency to come together for focused thought on family literacy." (Adult educator from a local community school).

Comments from the Statewide Invitational Conference

"The family shelter is interested in working with school age children and their parents together. We included family literacy as a component of our proposal for the homeless." (Coordinator).

"The urban school teams have encouraged local public schools to write Commonwealth In service Institute grants under Adult Education. Five grants were written." (Director, Program for Urban School Teams, Mass. Department of Education).

"Head Start has just ordered two books through conference material and using a wonderful poster received." (Head Start Coordinator).

"This was a great conference and an excellent way to meet other concerned educators. I sincerely hope one is planned for next year." (Representative from Public Broadcasting)

" The Adult Learning Center is interested in collaborating on a family literacy project with family shelters and have written a proposal". (Adult literacy specialist).

"I was very impressed with the quality of the speakers presenta tions. Very informative. Have put a lot of those ideas into practice with our families. They love them too!" (Even Start Coordinator).

"The literacy center, public library, local school department and United Way have established the need for a collaborative. The workshop I attended gave us the incentive to forge ahead". (Library literacy practitioner).

"It re-energized me to use fine children's literature with adult students who are parents and grandparents." (Reading Consultant).

"The quality of the presentations was sustained from beginning to end". (Director, community opportunity and training center).

"I am interested in initiating a Reach out and Read program (Dr. Needleman's program with hospitals). Infants and toddlers are an underserved population. What a wonderful intervention!" (Multicultural specialist for Even Start).

more, experience has proved that the typical, standard, post-conference evaluation forms frequently provide only superficial reactions to an event. The conference was so stimulating to both participants and planners alike that several weeks elapsed before a one page, post-conference questionnaire was sent to all attendees.

The post-conference mailing was successful in capturing the lingering impressions of both the CCFL participants and invited guests. A copy of the Handbook was offered as an incentive for completing and returning the questionnaire. We believe this was a factor in the high rate of return. The questionnaires were mailed in August—the height of the summer vacation period. Even so, 35 percent of questionnaires were returned. (See figures A.3. through A.5. for a summary of the results. The bar graphs illustrate the results.)

MID-PROJECT PROGRESS REPORT

This mid-project progress report requested participant teams to evaluate their progress in developing working relationships across agencies and to identify barriers and solutions that affected the local agenda (See CCFL Progress Report at end of Appendix A).

The results of the questionnaire were very revealing. It was obvious that, as a result of the family literacy conference, many participants had come away with new ideas which they wanted to incorporate into their final plans. On the other hand, some groups were having difficulty scheduling meetings during the mid-summer months when participation is less dependable because of vacations. Most respondents checked off the comment that "all things considered, our collaboration is working pretty well." It was interesting to read a somewhat discouraging mid-year progress report from one librarian who used the questionnaire to express her frustration with city budget cuts and general concerns about the library. However, five months later this same person communicated a more upbeat attitude in her personal interview with the project director. She remarked on the extremely positive effect of the CCFL project on the development of a new image for the library within the community.

Overall, the political and economic factors of the recession seemed to play havoc with all communities. The greatest barriers to a successful collaboration at this point in the process were:

- The impact of a loss of state aid to cities and towns across the Commonwealth.
- Stress on staff of all agencies who were stretched too thin.

POST-PROJECT ASSESSMENT

At the end of the project year, and before the final date for filing a Letter of Intent for LSCA funds, participant teams attended a halfday meeting to share events which occurred during the course of the project. This focus group was involved in a brainstorming session to create a list of benefits gained from CCFL participation, to discuss specific barriers in the development of their plans, and generally make several specific recommendations.

At this meeting, two communities shared the success stories of what had been happening on the local level. One of the Chapter One directors in concert with the collaborative group wrote and was funded for a federal Even Start award. Another group mentioned that one of the key players in the collaboration had received national recognition for its workplace literacy efforts.

Participants indicated the following indicators of success. The participants:

- Developed new tools for interagency planning.
- Promoted better ways to serve a shared target population through planning.
- Reduced isolation from other agencies.
- Developed a local network of service providers.
- Succeeded in getting state policymakers to make a commitment to family literacy.
- Provided materials and resources.
- Changed conceptions of service from an individual to a family focus.
- Provided confirmation to libraries about their role in service to families.
- Provided outreach strategies to different populations.
- Provided opportunities to share information about services (problems, ideas, dreams).

Letters of Intent

The letters of intent were the one page written commitments from communities which signaled their intention to formally apply for LSCA Title I funds for FY 1992. Each participating site was invited to submit such a letter to the MBLC by October 1991. However, submitting the letter of intent was not a condition for participation in the project itself.

In fact, five communities submitted a letter of intent to apply for LSCA Title I funds to the Massachusetts Board of Library Commissioners. This was evidence of "good faith" on the part of the programs, since the cycle is lengthy, and no immediate decisions on the success (or failure) to fund projects was possible until June, 1992. The Board had established a priority for family literacy proposals for 1992 as an incentive under the most recent supplement to its federally mandated Massachusetts Long Range Program 1991-96. Furthermore, two communities had made substantial progress in their collaboration and were able to submit a finished proposal for LSCA Title VI funds to meet the December, 1991 deadline. One of the two communities was successful in receiving an additional $35,000 to expand the project area to two other cities.

IN-DEPTH INTERVIEWS

In-depth interviews were conducted by the Project Director in two modes—either by an on-site visit or by extended telephone interviews after the official end of the project. In each case, several members of the community team were involved in the process. This information was incorporated into the Handbook.

FINAL PROPOSALS

Five of the six communities participating in this project submitted final proposals. Each proposal was based on the unique needs of the community and a specifically developed plan. Some of the family literacy objectives presented in the five proposals include the following:

Proposed Family Literacy Objectives:

- To hold at least 16 intergenerational activities for adults and their children (at the library) between February and June.
- To establish a core collection of library materials for families that will be ability and interest appropriate and to circulate at least 300 of these items by June of the project year.
- To establish a collection of at least 200 adult new reader and family reading materials in an area of the library designated as a Family Learning Center and to circulate each item at least once by the end of the project year.
- By the end of the project year, 90 percent of the parents involved in the project will read regularly to their children at home as measured by a locally prepared survey instrument.
- By the end of the project year, to host five parent workshops. Project participants will attend at least three of these special programs as measured by attendance records.
- By the end of the project year, 80 percent of parents involved will have demonstrated improved skills in reading to their children as documented by videotapes of initial and final sessions.
- By the final month of the project to develop at least 50 family reading kits for at-risk parents and children and to circulate these kits at least five times each.
- Beginning at the tenth month, set aside one day a week for two months to take the bookmobile to housing projects and family shelters to present programming and book exchange to at-risk families in conjunction with Even Start programs.
- To involve eight parents and children identified through Chapter One in a series of shared 12-week story hour sessions.
- To involve families in a series of workshops where they will attend separate parenting/storyhour sessions followed by shared parent/child activities.

An outcome of this project was the development of a collaborative spirit among those working at the state library agency and the Massachusetts Department of Education, as well as members of the community agencies, adult education providers, and the Massachusetts library community. With the leadership exercised by the state library agency came an obvious recognition of the need to be more inclusive of libraries as potential partners in family literacy planning.

Conclusion

The summer after the family literacy conference, the project director was invited to participate on the adult education committee of a comprehensive statewide assessment of educational needs in the Commonwealth. In the final document coordinated by the Naples Institute of Mt. Ida College, "The Massachusetts Educational Inventory: Facts, Issues and Options Regarding the Future of Education in Massachusetts," it was stated that "family literacy programs offer great potential because they are responsive to the needs of children, adults, and the family unit. Family literacy programs should be encouraged and expanded. A vehicle is needed to do this . . . The Massachusetts Board of Library Commissioners, and local libraries, should be encouraged to take leadership in this effort in collaboration with schools, community institutions, and other appropriate partners."

In late 1991, the Governor of the Commonwealth called for a re-structuring of education and created the new position of Secretary of Education with a mandate to oversee all education in the state. As a result of the educational inventory, the project director, educational consultant, and others interested in family literacy were able to meet and discuss the need for family literacy with the Secretary. Several paragraphs about the importance of family literacy were incorporated into the Governor's Educational Reform Bill which was issued in January, 1992.

The dedication of agencies and organizations providing coordinated literacy support services in Massachusetts has enabled us to make progress in serving the needs of adults and their families in a time when state and local budgets are being cut on a daily basis. The Massachusetts Board of Library Commissioners is committed to working to further develop literacy programs in libraries with a strong emphasis on local planning and interaction with our agency and other state organizations which can support this effort.

Members of the Massachusetts CCFL Teams:

The following were among the principal agency representatives who worked together on a collaborative project. The project contact is denoted by an asterisk (*).

Brockton

Margy Akilian, Adult Education Specialist, Brockton Family Literacy Program
* Linda Braun, Brockton Adult Learning Center
Patricia Adams, Early Childhood Education Specialist/Brockton Family Literacy Program
Carol Duhamel, Brockton Public Library

Fitchburg

* Elizabeth Watson, Director Fitchburg Public Library
Louise Carpenter, Literacy Volunteers of Montachusetts
Judith Ann Pregot, Mount Wachusetts Community College, Adult Education Program
Robert Ciuffetti, Director, Education and Training, Montachusetts Opportunity Council, Inc.
Margaret Farry, Coordinator Central Massachusetts, SABES (System of Adult Basic Education Support)

Greenfield

* Michael Francheschi, Greenfield Public Library
Ryan Murphy, Dial Self Program
Lindy Whiton, Greenfield Community College
Phil Rabinowitz, The Literacy Project

Peabody/Salem

Brendan Walsh, Salem Public Schools/Director, Chapter One
Sylvia Mulcahy, Salem Public Schools/Chapter One
* Mary Ann Tricarico, Peabody Institute Library
Marjorie Empacher, Salem State College
Phyllis Rantz, Chapter One, Peabody Public Schools

Somerville

* Ann Dausch, Supervisor, Children's Services, Somerville Public Library Schools
Pero, Director SCALE (Adult Learning Center) Somerville Public
Karen Lindberg, Early Childhood Supervisor
Susan Rabinowitz, Even Start Director, Somerville Public Schools
Maria Botehlo, Multicultural Literacy Links Project
Alberta Leach, Education Coordinator, CAAS-Headstart
Nomi Davidson, Somerville Even Start

Wareham

Susan Pizzolato, Wareham Free Public Library
Adelaide Gardner, Wareham Free Public Library
* Mary Jane Pillsbury, Director, Wareham Free Public Library
Patricia Moncey, Director Wareham Public Schools/Chapter One
John Amaral, Director, Wareham Adult Education Program

FIGURE A.6. Agenda for Planning Workshop

AGENDA FOR PLANNING WORKSHOP
Friday, December 14, 1990
Framingham Public Library
9:30 a.m. to 4:00 p.m.

	Activity	Time
I.	Coffee	9:30-10:00
II.	Introductions (S. Shelley Quezada) Goals and Agenda for the Day (Cristine Smith, World Education)	10:00-10:00
III.	Overview and Goals of the Project	10:15-10:30
IV.	Introductory Discussion on Family Literacy Rational, Typology (Dr. Ruth Nickse Consultant, Nickse Associates)	10:30-11:15
V.	First Steps in Needs & Resource Assessment: Community Mapping Exercise (in community groups) (Cristine Smith)	11:15-12:30
VI.	LUNCH: Informal grouping of ABE, School, Library and Support Service People (Provided by MBLC)	12:30-1:15
VII.	Description of Family Literacy Programs and Designs (Dr. Ruth Nickse)	1:15-2:30
VIII.	Next Steps: goal setting exercise, intro- duction to steps in planning process, setting up first meeting date and agenda, etc. (in community groups) (Cristine Smith)	2:30-3:30
	Sharing ideas with whole group generating list of materials or TA that community groups need from project staff (Cristine Smith)	3:30-3:45
IX.	Evaluation of Planning Workshops (Cristine Smith)	3:45-4:00

FIGURE A.7. Community Collaboration for Family Literacy

COMMUNITY COLLABORATIONS FOR FAMILY LITERACY

Local Site Meeting Record

Project Name: Location:

Recorder: Observer:

Date:

1. Agenda for Meeting Includes:

2. List of Participants Attending and/ Agency Represented:

3. Key Decisions Reached at this meeting include:

4. Achievements to date include:

5. Barriers to progress include:

6. Assignments for individuals/agencies and due dates includes:

7. Next meeting date, location and time:

8. List any informal meetings held or telephone contacts:

Other comments:

Thanks for contributing this information

FIGURE A.8. Statewide Invitational Conference

BUILDING COLLABORATIONS
FOR FAMILY LITERACY

A STATEWIDE INVITATIONAL CONFERENCE

Friday June 14, 1991   **8:30–4:00 p.m.**   **Bentley College, Waltham, MA**

You have been selected to participate in the first statewide conference which will provide a comprehensive overview of some of the most important issues in family literacy. This conference will convene a group of adult educators, librarians, Chapter One and local school personnel, family support service professionals and others interested in building a structure for family literacy at both state and local levels.

This conference will address:

- **Building collaborations to support family literacy**
- **Issues and models of practice in family literacy**
- **The role of federal and state funding in family literacy**
- **Federal and state policy on family literacy**

Working Sessions topics will include:

- **Emergent Literacy**
- **Design of Instruction and Assessment**
- **Research in Family Literacy**
- **Multicultural issues in Family Literacy**

Featured Keynote Speaker:

Thomas Sticht, Applied Behavior and Cognitive Sciences, El Cajon, California

The Intergenerational Transfer of Cognitive Skills: A Justification for Family Literacy?

FIGURE A.8 (cont'd)

Confirmed speakers:

Antonia Stone President Playing to Win on using computers for family math
A Representative from the National Center for Family Literacy in Louisville, Kentucky
Patty Edwards, Michigan State University, author of *Parents as Reading Partners*
David Dickinson, Clarke University, on emergent literacy
Gail Weinstein-Shr, U. Mass. Amherst, on multicultural issues in family literacy
Dick McLaughlin, Lawrence Public Library - about the Barbara Bush Foundation for Family Literacy Project
Ruth S. Nickse, speaking on the evaluation of family literacy projects
Eleanor Davis, Amesbury and Lorraine Burgoyne, Lowell - Program Directors of Massachusetts' *EVENSTART*
Gwen Morgan, Wheelock College, Boston, on building collaborations
Mary Reilly, Dorcas Place, Providence Rhode Island

This conference is supported in part by an LSCA Title VI grant to the Massachusetts Board of Library Commissioners and is offered by invitation to the Massachusetts community to enable building a statewide infrastructure for family literacy. We are collaborating with generous support from the Massachusetts Department of Education, Bureau of Adult Education; SABES, Quinsigamond Community College and Bentley College.

A registration fee of $20.00 includes a box luncheon, and coffee/tea breaks and free onsite parking.

Other conference bonuses include:

Special poster sessions presented by selected Massachusetts communities which are collaborating on family literacy projects

Selected exhibits will feature both print and non-print materials in support of family literacy

Information on EVENSTART, Reading is Fundamental, the Barbara Bush Foundation for Family Literacy and selected descriptions of other state and national projects will also be available.

Pre-registration is required because space is limited: Please tear off the reservation slip, enclose a check for $20.00 for each participant made payable to Quinsigamond Community College and return to : Shelley Quezada, Massachusetts Board of Library Commissioners, 648 Beacon St. Boston, MA 02215. Tel: (617)267-9400 or 1-800-952-7403.

Registration confirmation, program update and a map to conference site will be sent out in early June.

Building Collaborations for Family Literacy Conference

Name:_____ Title:_____

Agency/Organization:_____

Address:_____

City:_____ State:_____ Zip:_____

Phone: (   ) _____

FIGURE A.9. Statewide Invitational Conference

BUILDING COLLABORATIONS FOR FAMILY LITERACY

A Statewide Invitational Conference

June 14, 1991
Graduate Center
Bentley College, Waltham, MA

This conference on "building collaborations" is made possible with strong support of public/private organizations and institutions. It is cosponsored by the "Service Learning Project" at Bentley College. It has been generously supported by the Massachusetts Department of Education, Bureau of Adult Education and the System for Adult Basic Education Support (SABES) Centers. Quinsigamond Community College has generously acted as fiscal agent. Funding is provided in part by an LSCA Title VI grant from the Office of Educational Research and Improvement (OERI), U.S. Department of Education and administered by the Massachusetts Board of Library Commissioners.

Project Coordinator: Shelley Quezada, Massachusetts Board of Library Commissioners, 648 Beacon St. Boston, MA 02115 (617) 267-9400

Project Consultant: Ruth S. Nickse, Nickse Associates

Lea McGee, Boston College, Chestnut Hill, MA.
"Using Environmental Print to Initiate Beginning Reading with Children" Room 141

Robert Needleman, M.D., Boston City Hospital, Boston, MA *"Reach out and Read: Using the Pediatric Clinic to Support Literacy With At Risk Families"* Room 160

Elizabeth Stahl, Wheelock College, Boston, MA *"Stride Rite Intergenerational Project: A Public/Private Partnership"* Room: 143

CLOSING PLENARY SESSION: 2:45-3:30 p.m. The Pavilion

"Issues and Concerns in Family Literacy: Developing a Vision for Massachusetts"

Commissioner Harold Raynolds Jr., Massachusetts Department of Education
Thomas Sticht, Applied Behavioral and Cognitive Sciences
Robert Spillman, National Center for Family Literacy
Patricia Edwards, Michigan State University
Elisabeth Twomey, Associate Commissioner for School Programs, Massachusetts Department of Education
Robert Bickerton, Director, Bureau of Adult Education, Massachusetts Department of Education
Linda Braun, Program Director, Brockton Adult Learning Center, Family Learning Program, Brockton, MA
Ruth S. Nickse, Nickse Associates, Moderator

WRAP-UP and AUDIENCE QUESTIONS 3:30-3:45 p.m.

3:45-4:30 p.m. POST-CONFERENCE RECEPTION (Registration area)

FIGURE A.9 (con'd)

Registration and Coffee
8:00- 9:00 a.m.

PLENARY SESSION: 9:00- 9:50 a.m.
                          The Pavilion

Welcome: Philip Friedman, Provost, Bentley College

KEYNOTE ADDRESS:
"The Intergenerational Transfer of Cognitive Skills:
A Justification for Family Literacy?"
Thomas Sticht, Applied Behavioral and Cognitive Sciences,
Inc., El Cajon, CA

CONCURRENT SESSIONS: 10:00 - 10:50 a.m.

Patricia Edwards, Michigan State University, Lansing, MI
"Building Collaborative Working Relations with Non-
Mainstream Parents, and Children: A Discussion of
Parents as Partners in Reading"   Room: The Pavilion

Antonia Stone: President, Playing to Win, New York City
"Parents, Kids and Computers"   Room 160

Shell Wortis and Lynne Hall: Literacy Connection,
Cambridge Public Schools, "Using Whole Language
Materials in the Multicultural Classroom"   Room 143

Mary Reilly, Director, Dorcas Place, Providence, RI
Lili Snelckus, Coordinator of Students
"Dorcas Place: a Holistic Learning Center Addressing
the Needs of Single Parent Families"   Room 141

CONCURRENT SESSIONS: 11:00 - 11:50 a.m.

David Dickinson, Clarke University, Worcester, MA
"Sowing the Seeds of Literacy: Supporting Early Literacy
Through Oral Language Experiences in Home and School"
                       Room: The Pavilion

Ruth S. Nickse, President, Nickse Associates, Brookline,
MA "A Typology for Family and Intergenerational Literacy
Programs: Implications for Evaluation"   Room 160

Gail Weinstein-Shr, University of Massachusetts, Amherst,
MA " Using Students' Stories to Link the Generations in
Multilingual Communities "   Room 143

Mary Jane Schmidt, Massachusetts Dept. of Education,
Bureau of Adult Education; Esther Leonelli and Linda
Huntington, Community Learning Center, Cambridge
"Family Literacy: Don't Forget Family Math!"   Room 141

LUNCH 12:00 - 12:45 p.m.

Box lunches will be served in the Registration Area.

PLEASE TAKE THIS OPPORTUNITY TO VISIT:
Rooms 164-161-163

POSTER SESSIONS: Descriptions of Family
Literacy/EVENSTART Projects. Project staff will be available during lunch to answer questions. A wealth of hand-
outs/information will be available in the poster/exhibit area.

EXHIBITS: The following selected publishers' exhibits
focus on family literacy activities and have helped support
this conference: Children's Press, Curriculum Associates,
Educator's Publishing Service, Jostens Learning Corporation, New Reader's Press. (Room 164)

VIDEOS: Featured videos of interest to family literacy
programs will be shown in the exhibit area (Room 164)
during registration and lunch.

AFTERNOON PLENARY SESSION: 12:50 - 1:40p.m.
                             The Pavilion

Featured speakers:

Robert E. Spillman, Vice-President, National Center for
Family Literacy, Louisville Kentucky.
"Developing Collaborations for Family Literacy: A National
Perspective"

Mary Haggerty, Program Coordinator, Reading is Fundamental, Washington, D.C.
"Reading is Fundamental to Family Literacy"

CONCURRENT SESSIONS: 1:45 - 2:40 p.m

Richard McLaughlin, Project Director, Lawrence Public
Library, Lawrence, MA, Teresa Williams, Literacy
Specialist and Antonia Jain, Children's Assistant,
"The Newcomer Family Literacy Program- a Barbara Bush
Foundation for Family Literacy Project"
                          Room: The Commons (3rd Floor)

CCFL PROGRESS REPORT

Thanks for taking time to answer this brief progress report on the Community Collaborations for Family Literacy Project. The information you provide will help us to better understand your needs in a collaborative project like this, which is a new experience for most of us. Please return completed Progress Reports to Shelley Quezada in the envelope provided by August 6th. Write additional information on the back or attach sheets--- the more we know, the faster we learn!!

1. How would you rate your community's progress to date in the CCFL project? Cheek which term describes your situation.

        _____ Just getting started with collaboration
        _____ Working out the kinks in our collaboration
        _____ All things considered, our collaboration is working well
        _____ All things considered, our collaboration is terrific
        _____ No noticeable progress in our collaboration

Comments:
_____
_____
_____

2. Rate the helpfulness of the following formal and informal CCFL events to your community's project. Write "1" for most helpful event, "2" for next helpful, and so until you rate an event as "7" for least important.
        _____ December training workshop
        _____ Visits of CCFL staff to your community
        _____ Other contacts with CCFL staff
        _____ June Family Literacy Conference
        _____ Interactions with local collaborators
        _____ Interactions with others interested in family literacy
        _____ Other, please explain

Comments:
_____
_____
_____

3. What did your collaboration get out of the June Conference? Check all that apply.

        ____ More information on collaborations
        ____ More information on family literacy
        ____ New contacts
        ____ Direction, guidance for our project
        ____ New ideas
        ____ Useful materials
        ____ Information on funding sources
        ____ Inspiration, courage to continue

Comments:_____
_____
_____

4. List one or two actions your collaboration will take as a result of the conference.
_____
_____
_____

5. List two or three main achievements your collaboration has accomplished to date._____
_____
_____

6. List any current or potential barriers in your community to collaboration and the family literacy agenda. _____
_____
_____

7. What help (information, resources) do you as a collaboration need to reach your community's goals for the CCFL project?
_____
_____
_____

8. Do you think that developing some sort of handbook about collaboration in family literacy based on this project's experience is (check your reaction)

_____ A dynamite idea
_____ An ok idea
_____ Not a good idea

Additional comments:

_____
_____
_____
_____
_____

APPENDIX B

UNITED WAY LITERACY SERVICE PROVIDERS SURVEY

United Way of _____ , as part of
an adult-literacy initiative, is conducting a study of literacy needs in our community. The results will guide the development of an action agenda tailored to
our community. (Indicate how United Way will use this survey information, and
what the benefit to the agency will be for participating.)

A volunteer will call to interview you.

Please complete the following items, providing your best estimates where
actual numbers are not known. If you have no information from which to estimate, please write "DK" indicating you do not know.

Name of Agency _____

Name of Literacy Program _____

Mailing Address _____

_____ ZIP Code _____

Telephone No. (_____) _____

Number of Sites Where Services Are Provided _____
(Please provide a list of addresses of all of your sites. This may be done on the reverse side.)

Name of Person Completing Survey _____

Title _____

Date _____

1. What type of literacy services do you offer?

   ☐ Basic Literacy only   ☐ ABE & ESL
   ☐ ABE (Adult Basic Ed) only   ☐ Basic Math
   ☐ ESL (English as Second   ☐ Other _____
       Language) only

2. Approximately how many individuals did you serve in 19 ____?

   _____ (enter number)   _____ % Male   _____ % Female

3. Approximately how many individuals do you serve in an average week?

   _____

4. Do you maintain information on the demographic characteristics, such as
   age and race, of your clients?

   ☐ Yes   ☐ No

5. Approximately what percentage of individuals served were in the following age groups?

_____ % 15–19 years   _____ % 20–24 years   _____ % 25–34 years

_____ % 35–59 years   _____ % 60 years and older

6. Approximately what percentage of individuals served were in the following groups?

_____ % African American   _____ % Asian/Pacific Islander

_____ % Caucasian   _____ % Hispanic   _____ % Native American

_____ % Other, please specify _____

7. In what ZIP code areas or community neighborhoods do most of your clients reside?

_____

8. When are your services available? (Check all that apply.)

☐ Daytime Hours   ☐ Monday–Friday   ☐ Sundays
☐ Evening Hours   ☐ Saturdays   ☐ Individually Determined
☐ Other, please specify _____

9. Are there any charges for your services or for the materials used?

☐ Yes   ☐ No

If yes:

a. What is your fee structure? _____

b. Do you provide financial assistance?   ☐ Yes   ☐ No

10. Are there eligibility criteria for your services?   ☐ Yes   ☐ No

If yes, check all that apply:
☐ Residency   ☐ Income
☐ Age   ☐ Participation in other social service program
☐ Other, please specify _____

11. Is there currently a waiting list for your services?

☐ Yes   ☐ No

If yes, approximately how long must an individual wait for service?

_____ Days   _____ Weeks   _____ Months

How many individuals are currently on your waiting list? _____

Do you refer clients to other literacy services if your services are not appropriate?

_____

If your waiting list is too long? _____

12. What instructional methods do you use? (Check all that apply.)

☐ One-to-one tutoring   ☐ Small group/average class
☐ Large group/class   size: _____
   instruction   ☐ Computer-assisted instruction (CAI)

If more than one method is checked, which is your primary method?

_____

13. What methods do you use to evaluate the progress of individuals in your program? (Check all that apply.)

☐ Completion of workbooks/materials
☐ Analysis of clinical test/evaluations
☐ Performance on objective/written test
☐ Reports by tutors
☐ Mastery of life coping/life maintenance skills
☐ Achievement of individually determined objectives
☐ Other, please specify _____

14. Do you have a follow-up procedure for individuals who complete your program?

☐ Yes   ☐ No

If yes, explain your method _____

_____

15. Do you have a follow-up procedure for individuals who do *not* complete your program?

☐ Yes   ☐ No

If yes, explain your method and the time frame for follow-up (one month, three months, etc.)

_____

_____

_____

16. What factors may prevent individuals from using your services? (Check all that apply.)

☐ Time/day services offered   ☐ Lack of awareness of service
☐ Fees or material costs   ☐ Stigma of illiteracy
☐ Other eligibility requirements ☐ Lack of child care
☐ Location of services   ☐ Lack of transportation
☐ Other, please specify _____

17. What percentage of your students/clients leaves your program without completing it?

_____ %

18. What would you estimate is the most common reason students leave without completing? (You may check more than one, but please put an asterisk (*) before the most common one.)

☐ Moved   ☐ Got a job
☐ Child care problems   ☐ Program did not meet needs
☐ Transportation   ☐ Lack of motivation
☐ Personal problems   ☐ Lack of success in program
☐ Illness/health   ☐ Needed more individualized help
☐ Skills too low   ☐ Unknown

19. Do you survey your clients on their experience with your program or do you have other means of obtaining feedback from them?

☐ Yes   ☐ No

20. How many paid staff persons work in your program?

_____ Full-time   _____ Part-time

What minimum qualifications/credentials do you require? _____

_____

_____

21. How many volunteers assist your program?

_____ Full-time   _____ Part-time

What minimum qualifications/credentials do you require? _____

_____

_____

22. Are many volunteers former students?   ☐ Yes   ☐ No

23. a. Do you provide orientation (initial introduction of the goals and methods of your program) for your paid staff?

☐ Yes   ☐ No

If yes, what kind and length of training are offered? _____

_____

b. Do you provide orientation for your volunteers?   ☐ Yes   ☐ No

If yes, what kind and length of training are offered? _____

_____

24. a. Do you provide ongoing in-service training for your paid staff?

☐ Yes   ☐ No

If yes, what kind and length of training are offered? _____

_____

24. b. Do you provide ongoing in-service training for your volunteers?

☐ Yes   ☐ No

If yes, what kind and length of training are offered? _____

_____

25. Which of the following resources do you need to make your literacy program more successful? (Check all that apply.)

☐ Curriculum design
☐ Paid professional staff
☐ Volunteer training
☐ Financial support
☐ Identification of those needing services
☐ Technical and administrative support
☐ Evaluation and testing of learners
☐ Bilingual tutors
☐ Other, please specify _____

☐ Educational materials
☐ Volunteers
☐ Staff training
☐ Outreach & promotion
☐ Child care
☐ Volunteer training
☐ Sites for tutoring/workshops
☐ Incentive programs
☐ Transportation

26. Which of the following resources would you share with other literacy programs? (Check all that apply.)

☐ Curriculum design
☐ Volunteer training
☐ Technical/administrative support
☐ Evaluation/testing devices
☐ Bilingual tutors
☐ Transportation
☐ Other, please specify _____

☐ Educational materials
☐ Volunteers
☐ Ongoing/training
☐ Child care
☐ Sites for tutoring/ workshops

27. If an individual in your program needs other assistance, which of the following services do you provide, if any? Please indicate in column A below.

If these services are unavailable through your organization, please indicate in column B those services, if any, for which you make referrals. (Check all that apply.)

Service Area	A. Provides	B. Refers
Career Counseling	☐	☐
Child care	☐	☐
Consumer affairs	☐	☐
Crisis intervention	☐	☐
Educational and vocational training	☐	☐
Emergency assistance	☐	☐
Employment placement/training	☐	☐

27.—continued

Service Area	A. Provides	B. Refers
Family and marital counseling	☐	☐
Financial assistance	☐	☐
Food	☐	☐
Housing and shelter	☐	☐
Legal assistance	☐	☐
Medical assistance	☐	☐
Mental health assistance	☐	☐
Older-adult services	☐	☐
Recreational services	☐	☐
Religious services/training	☐	☐
Substance abuse assistance	☐	☐
Utilities assistance	☐	☐
Workplace literacy programming	☐	☐
Youth services	☐	☐
Other (specify) _____	☐	☐

28. What is your annual budget? _____ ;

What are primary sources of funds? _____

_____

29. What are your major funding challenges? _____

_____

_____

30. What role do you recommend for United Way in addressing the need for literacy?

_____

_____

_____

_____

SURVEY OF LITERACY NEEDS FOR SOCIAL SERVICE AGENCIES
(Public and Private Sector)

United Way of _____ , as part of an adult-literacy initiative, is conducting a study of literacy needs in our community. The results will guide the development of an action agenda tailored to our community. Your reponses to this survey will be held in confidence.

Please complete the following items, providing your best estimates where actual numbers are not known. If you have no information from which to estimate, please write "DK" indicating you do not know.

1. Approximately how many individuals did you serve in 19 _____?

2. Among your clientele, are there individuals who have difficulty filling out required forms?

   ☐ Yes   ☐ No   ☐ DK

   If yes, approximately what percent have this difficulty? _____

3. Among your clientele, are there individuals who do not speak English well?

   ☐ Yes   ☐ No   ☐ DK

   If yes, approximately what percentage have this difficulty? _____

4. Do you make referrals to your clients for literacy services?

   ☐ Yes   ☐ No   ☐ DK

   If yes, please list those places to which you refer clients:

   _____

   _____

   Do you know of other service providers to whom you might refer clients?

   ☐ Yes   ☐ No

   If yes, please name these providers:

   _____

   _____

5. Do you have information on the approximate number of your clients who are presently receiving some form of literacy instruction?

   ☐ Yes   ☐ No

   If yes, what is this number? _____

6. In your opinion, how many of your clients who need literacy services would be interested in receiving literacy instruction if it were made readily available?

_____

7. Which of the following might clients of your program perceive as barriers to participation in an adult literacy program? (Please check all that apply.)

☐ Time/day services offered   ☐ Language barrier
☐ Fees or material costs   ☐ Lack of awareness of service
☐ Eligibility requirement   ☐ Stigma of illiteracy
☐ Location of services   ☐ Child care
☐ Privacy issue   ☐ Transportation
☐ Other, please specify _____

8. Are you currently providing funding or other resources to support literacy services?

_____

If yes, please describe _____

9. What role do you recommend for United Way in addressing the need for literacy?

_____

_____

_____

_____

Name of Agency _____

Agency Address _____

_____ ZIP Code _____

Agency Telephone No. (_____) _____

Name of Person Completing Survey _____

Title _____

Please return the completed survey to: Jane Smith, United Way of Anytown, 123 Main Street, Anytown, USA.

THANK YOU.

APPENDIX C

Sample Proposal

LAWRENCE PUBLIC LIBRARY
BARBARA BUSH FOUNDATION/
FAMILY LITERACY

Program Narrative:

1. Organization's Background and the Need for the Project:

Lawrence, Massachusetts, known as "The Immigrant City," has throughout its history been dealing with the unique problem of educating wave after wave of newly arrived immigrants of diverse ethnic and linguistic backgrounds. Currently the school department's bilingual education department is providing instruction in sixteen languages. Many of these recently arrived immigrants are from a rural society, coming with little or no formal education to the city with its complex urban problems. They must overcome the dual problems of learning a new language and acquiring much needed literacy skills. In a special report on the Merrimack Valley's illiteracy problem, the Pulitzer-Prize-winning Lawrence Eagle-Tribune reported that more than 30,000 adults in Lawrence and surrounding communities are believed to be illiterate. Statistics quoted in Mayor Kevin J. Sullivan's proposal to develop a literacy coalition for the city of Lawrence, based on the June 1987 city census, indicate that 25% of the 63,175 residents of the city of Lawrence are of Hispanic origin (informal estimates range as high as 35%.) This is an increase of over 9% above the figures in the 1980 federal census. Of the 9,800 students enrolled in public schools during 1987, 63% are minorities, with the majority being Hispanics whose primary language is not English. The Lawrence School Department released figures indicating that 90% of this school year's first-graders are Hispanic. There are 25,094 adults 25 years of age or older in Lawrence who lack a high school diploma. The dropout rate for Lawrence High School is nearly 50% with approximately 20% disappearing between freshman and sophomore years. An additional 20% attrition occurs between sophomore and junior years of high school. Considering the fact that literacy problems are compounded by the bilingual/bicultural nature of our population, these figures indicate that the estimated national average of 30% of the population being functionally illiterate is exceeded in Lawrence.

As a member of the Lower Merrimack Valley Literacy Coalition and the Massachusetts Coalition for Adult Literacy, the Lawrence Public Library is working to provide literacy support to both adult and children in the community. Our most recent experience includes providing literacy programming that meet the needs of both generations. We have successfully piloted an intergenerational literacy project with assistance from local providers and are currently running an LSCA Title I "Library Family Literacy Project," which provides similar services to the community on an evening schedule. Additionally we have implemented an LSCA Title VI Library Literacy Project, which provides a fully equipped, computer-based literacy support lab to the community.

In April, the Lawrence Public Library was honored by the Lower Merrimack Valley Private Industry Council for outstanding leadership in community and workplace literacy. We are currently providing classroom instruction for 35 adults and literacy-oriented activities for 12 children. Our computer-equipped Literacy Lab is being used by hundreds of people during the month as other adult education providers bring their students to the library to use the facility when the space is available. Both of these projects will end on September 30, 1990, without additional support.

2. Project Purpose and Objectives: This program is designed to meet children's needs by providing parents with support enabling them to read to their children while improving their own literacy and parenting skills. By doing so, the damaging cycle of intergenerational illiteracy can be broken. If funded, this project will enable the Lawrence Public Library to empower more new readers in our community by providing service, space and materials to meet the needs of families in Lawrence who identify themselves as needing literacy support.

Goals:

- To provide an intergenerational literacy program for adults and their children which enhances opportunities for basic literacy instruction.
- To maintain a microcomputer-assisted literacy lab which provides tutor recruitment and training, and supervision for intergenerational literacy instruction.

Objectives:

- Within one year, to provide 16 parents on a 0-6th grade level with a computer-assisted literacy program using volunteer tutors.
- Within one year, to enable 16 parents to advance one grade level in reading and writing skills as measured by an Informal Reading Inventory, standardized testing and teacher evaluation.
- Within one year, to enable 5 adults to enter further education or skills training.
- Within one year, to provide on-going Read-Aloud workshops for 32 participants (parents and their children).
- Within one year, to provide 16 children with a rich on-goinng read-aloud experience.
- Within one year, to increase New Readers at the Lawrence Public Library section by at least 100 volumes.
- Within one year to evaluate the newly purchased materials in the New Readers collection and to make those evaluations available to ABE practitioners in the area.
- Within one year, to develop locally relevant, intergenerational literacy materials in-house, using desk-top publishing hardware/software.

- Within one year, to develop locally relevant, intergenerational literacy materials in-house, using desk-top publishing hardware/software.
- Within one year, to increase usage of the Lawrence Public Library by 16 new readers and their families.

3. Project Design: Classes will be held from 9:00 a.m. to 12:00 noon, Tuesdays and Thursdays in the Adult Literacy Support Lab, with all students gathered for attendance and announcements. The group will then divide: approximately half of the 0-6th-grade-level readers will remain in the classroom for a "stand-up-lesson" from the literacy specialist, while the remaining students will be assisted by tutors at the computer for computer-assisted instruction or language experiencne writing, or at desks and tables located in various parts of the library for one-on-one tutoring. The children will work with the parents on family histories or other joint activities or adjourn to the Children's Room for appropriate programming with the Children's Room Library Assistant. Approximate exercises developed by the combined staff will provide the family with unique opportunities to develop family histories together for eventual in-class publication.

Stand-up lessons will vary, but normally will include a warm-up period of focussed discussion of current events or students' work in progress; a brief phonics lesson with opportunities for both oral and written drill; and an exercise in reading comprehension which might consist of stories from the newspaper (re-written for the student's reading level) or poetry. Additional lessons may involve following written directions for making a greeting card or Christmas ornament, or for performing a simple science experiment using household materials. It is important that the reading lessons be rich in subject matter as well as skills development because adult non-readers need to acquire a foundation about the culture around them. This will not only improve their reading; it will also improve their chances for educational success later.

At 10:30 a.m., after a short break, the group will switch and divide again; those students who have been working one-on-one with their tutors will come together for a group lesson. Those who have received the earlier group lesson will begin to work with their tutors. Classes will end at 12:00 noon.

There will be a great deal of variation in the work students do with their tutors. For each student, an outline of specific instructional goals will be designed by the literacy specialist and the tutor, with attention to decoding strengths and weaknesses, comprehension skills, spelling and writing. It will also include whatever personal functional goals students may have, such as passing the driver's license test, learning how to fill out job applications, or being able to read to their children.

Key to this project is our understanding of how the composing process works, and hands-on experience using the computer/word processor as a tool in the teaching of writing. Tutors and students will create language experience stories together, enter them on the computer, and practice reading them from printed copy. These stories will also serve as sources of spelling and vocabulary words referred to as the "write-to read" approach, not only helps alleviate the problem of the paucity of adult basic reading material, it virtually guarantees that what is read will be personally relevant to the student.

4. Project Staff: The grant will be administrated by Richard McLaughlin, Lawrence Public Library Assistant Director, member of the Commonwealth Literacy Corps's Library Literacy Advisory Group, member of the Massachusetts Department of Education/Massachusetts Coalition for Adult Literacy-Adult Education Funding Task Force. (See attached resume.)

The part-time Literacy Specialist to be hired under the grant will be responsible for all educational aspects of the project, including recruiting, training, and supervising volunteer tutors, recruiting and testing students, ordering materials, reporting on a quarterly basis to the Advisory Board and familiarizing library adult services staff with all aspects of the Adult Literacy Support Lab, with special attention to materials, computer hardware and software. (See attached job description.)

The Part-time Children's Room Library Assistant to be hired under the grant will be responsible for providing prereading activities for children in the Family Literacy Project during class hours and will work closely with the Literacy Specialist to coordinate intergenerational activities, such as family histories.

5. Project Evaluation: The members of the Lawrence Literacy Coalition have agreed to act as a community-based Advisory Board. It will be the task of the board members to meet quarterly in order to review the performance of the project. Brief written reports will be submitted to the board detailing enrollments, student progress as measured by standardized tests, the results of qualitative student evaluations of the program (see below), and the content of in-service tutor training during the previous quarter.

Intake testing for new students will be kept to a minimum because for many adult non-readers, testing symbolizes failure and humiliation. Accordingly, we will use modified testing procedures which have been designed to be as streamlined as possible, while still offering an adequate measure of entering grade level and adequate screening procedures for detecting possible learning disabilities. These procedures contain subject matter for reading and writing that is keyed to adult interest.

On-going student progress will be evaluated quarterly, using the following standardized tests at the instructor's discretion: ABLE, Stanford Reading Comprehension, Gates MacGinity and Metropolitan Achievement (reading). (Since these latter three tests were designed for children and are not accurately normed for adults, their results can only be interpreted comparatively to show relative progress. They cannot be considered as a precise measure of grade level.) The above tests will also be used to indicate areas of strength and weakness in order to modify students' individual instructional plans. Finally, where indicated, students will be given specialized tests to determine the nature and extent of any learning disabilities.

Quarterly testing will also serve to make students more familiar with standardized tests and strategies for successful test taking. Such tests are frequently used for admission to job training programs and are being used with increasing frequency by employers.

An individual instructional plan for each student will be designed by the literacy specialist, the tutor, and the student, meeting in conference. Each plan will contain realistic timetables for mastering specific decoding, reading comprehension, spelling and writing skills. It will also contain a list of the student's short-term personal goals, such as learning to write a telephone message, or reading the street signs, with appropriate timetables for these goals as well. This plan will be kept in the student's folder for the tutor's ready reference and as a qualitative way of monitoring each student's progress.

Near the end of every Tuesday and Thursday session, students and tutors will summarize in a sentence or two in the students' journal what he or she learned that evening. This technique is designed to encourage the important reading and writing skill of summarizing, and to help the student monitor his or her own progress. It is also a way to encourage students to reflect on each night's work and to evaluate their performance and that of the teacher and tutor.

Three times a year, in December, March and June, students will be asked to respond to a brief questionnaire evaluating the project, including teaching effectiveness, staff responsiveness, materials used and physical layout. Students who cannot write easily will be aided by tutors. These questionnaires would then be made available to the Advisory Board to help in its overall evaluation and recommendations.

6. Project Site: The Lawrence Public Library will serve as the project site. The Newcomer Family Literacy Project will have unlimited access to our Literacy Support lab, a relaxed learning environment equipped with 7 Apple Ilgs computers. Additional computers are available in the Children's Room. In addition. literacy oriented software, books and audio/visual materials are available for use by learners, literacy volunteers, and other literacy providers in the community. This space is available during all library operational hours, including three evenings until 9:00 p.m., and Saturday and Sunday afternoons. It is precisely this availability that makes the library a unique and appropriate location as a community adult literacy support facility.

The Lawrence Public Library has placed the highest priority on developing a relevant collection and organizing relevant services for the multi-ethnic community of Lawrence. We have an up-to-date collection that reflects the cultural heritages and minority characteristics of the city. We have a bilingual/bicultural professional staff with a thorough understanding of and sensitivity to the factor of ethnicity in the heritage, behavior and lifestyles of the people in the Lawrence community. We house an English as a Second Language Teacher's Collection, and we are a Library Literacy Resource Center for the Commonwealth Literacy Corps and serve as the Massachusetts Department of Education System for Adult Basic Education Support (SABES) Northeast Regional Resource Center.

7. Community Support: The Lawrence Public Library is located in the heart of the city, within walking distance from all of the social service agencies and many of the area's churches, which are essential resources in providing information and referrals in a continuous outreach effort. In addition, we already enjoy a very special relationship with the city's literacy providers and educational institutions in the community.

The Northern Essex Community College (NECC) Lawrence Campus is based in our facility and has brought over 3000 adults through our doors in the first two years of the program. Over 2,190 of these people became program participants; an additional 600 have attended classes in our building within this past year.

The vast majority of these participants are limited-English-speaking adults with low education levels. We have a mutually beneficial system of referral between our agencies. NECC has a waiting list of over 250 students, with priority given to those with at least 8 years of education in their native country. We focus our services on those NECC is unable to serve.

The Lawrence Public Library has a strong working relationship with the Lawrence School Department's Adult Learning Center, the community's social service agencies and the many fine adult education providers in Lawrence who make up the Lawrence Literacy Coalition.

We collaborate with the Lawrence School Department's Adult Leaning Center Literacy Volunteers Project, providing space and materials for tutors and their students. The Lawrence Read-Aloud Program, sponsored by the Library, the Lawrence School Department and the Chamber of Commerce's Business/Education Collaborative, is administered through the library. This program recruits and coordinates volunteers from the business community to read to youngsters in grades K through 3, thus promoting reading at an early age by providing role models in the literacy experience.

8. Future Funding: The Lawrence Public Library is committed to the continued provision of literacy support for those in need and will request increased general funds from the City of Lawrence for a Literacy Specialist and for software, materials, supplies and other expenses. Our goal is to establish the Newcomer Family Literacy Project as a regular on-going program within our library.

The eventual plan is to staff the project totally with library personnel, in particular with an experienced librarian who has considerable training and expertise in literacy. Continued training will be acquired through participation in classes at local universities and colleges, as well as through workshops provided by SABES.

9. Budget: The total $25,000 budget requested will be augmented by an additional $11,500 in locally appropirated funds and in-kind services. Of these funds $7,000 represent in-kind commitment from existing library staff. An additional $4,500 will be spent on library materials, computer software, telephone, postage, advertising, and miscellaneous expenses.

Soar to New Heights Through Knowledge

Lawrence Public Library

Barbara Bush Foundation for Family Literacy
Newcomer Family Literacy Project
Update
June, 1991

Project Director: Richard McLaughlin
Literacy Specialist: Teresa Williams
Literacy Assistant: Antonia Jain

Recruiting and Interviewing: Prior to hiring project staff, recruitment was initiated by the Project Director through Lower Merrimack Valley Literacy Coalition member agencies whose referrals provided an overwhelming potential class list. Initially, 45 potential students were interviewed and evaluated, and of those, 18 adults with a total of 12 children were selected for class participation. Recruitment is done on a continuing basis both through Literacy Coalition member and other agency referrals and through unsolicited walk-ins. Our target population consists of non-English speaking adults with less than a sixth grade education in their native language. We further focus on individuals with little or no education in the United States.

Staff Training: The Project Director and Literacy Specialists attend workshops provided by SABES, the Mass. Department of Education's System for Adult Basic Education Support.

Instructional activities: Instructional activities for parents and children are coordinated so that learned experiences can be shared and reinforced in the home. For example, if parents are learning greetings or to identify parts of the body, the children will learn the same concept at their own level, through stories, games and art projects.

We use the whole language approach with students developing stories as a group. Stories are typed and distributed for reading and vocabulary is drawn from the story. Each student has a notebook and keeps a daily journal describing their activities and accomplishments in class. The class time for parents and children consists of story hours, arts and craft, and other joint activities such as baking cookies, which we believe reinforces the importance of parental interaction with children.

In addition, Parents and children receive an introduction to the computer both one-on-one and as a group. The students are building data files for family histories and each has a data disk for saving this work. Some students also use the computers to develop resumés and write letters to family and friends.

The most popular software program in our class is "Print Shop," which students use to make cards, signs, banners and T-Shirts. Closely following in popularity are a number of programs from the "Talking Schoolhouse" series produced by Orange Cherry Software. We have found that using the computers for fun class projects gives the students a sense of empowerment and helps to foster group development that extends beyond the classroom.

Parent Child /Activity and Special Events: Classroom activities for the children are in both English and Spanish, with emphasis on learning English. Our intent is to teach English to help the children prepare for school and to improve their ability to function in an English-speaking society. However, because Spanish is the spoken language in the home, and to help preserve heritage, as well as for convenience it is also used in the classroom setting.

An essential part of our program is the process of familiarizing parents and their children with the use of the library. All students and parents have received library orientation and have been issued library cards.

Curriculum is developed to accommodate the seasons and various holidays. For example, Both children and parents learned about Christmas customs, shared their knowledge and wrote stories. Parents learned about traditional Christmas foods by practicing reading recipes. The joint activity involved preparation of Christmas cookies by parents and children together.

Parents and children were asked to identify various foods before eating them at the Thanksgiving party. For Valentines Day, the group again made cookies together, learning about kitchen appliances and measuring. Both parents and children made Christmas cards cards for family and friends. In March, students wrote stories about Easter and Easter traditions from various countries was highlighted. All participants dyed Easter eggs and made Easter baskets. This was a new experience for everybody.

Parents were provided with workshops by Mary Wesson, a representative of the School Department's Parent Information Center and George Edmonds, Director of the Lawrence Read Aloud Program, and Leslie Kalafaski of the Lawrence School Department, as well as library staff members. Parents are enthusiastic about these activities and most are reading to their children at home on a regular basis. An information session regarding registering children for school was also provided by the School Department.

Problems Encountered: Realizing that we are dealing with a highly mobile population, we initially over-enrolled the class with the hope of maintaining a class size that would be optimal. Furthermore, the constant turn-over in students has kept the curriculum in constant adjustment. Instructional activities are often repeated and lessons reviewed to meet the needs of all students.

One of the most difficult problem to overcome is the inconsistency of attendance by the children. Parents leave children at home for any number of reasons, even though they realize the class is for both parents and children. It is difficult to plan activities for children when we're unsure of the age-group for any particular day.

We try to be flexible in meeting the needs of the children. The result is that although we aim our program at children between the ages of 2 and 6, we will end up with younger or older children depending on circumstances. For example child care problems may result in a parent bringing in an infant, for which they must assume responsibility or school vacation scheduling may result in an influx of older siblings. When ever possible we adapt the program to meet the needs of our students. In cases where a younger child is disruptive, however, the parent is asked to leave the area. This is a very rare occurrence. Our overall experience has been that we can deal with each new problem as it arises.

For more information:
Richard C. McLaughlin
Lawrence Public Library
51 Lawrence St.
Lawrence, Ma
01841

APPENDIX D

Federal Legislation in Support of Family Literacy

Federal dollars in support of family literacy are appropriated through a number of legislative programs. These programs provide opportunities for parents and children to work together to improve their academic skills. A number of programs provide parenting and early childhood opportunities. All programs require cooperation between adult education and early childhood education.

FEDERAL LEGISLATION	FUNDING	CONTACT
Adult Education Act. P.L. 100-297, as amended by the National Literacy Act of 1991, Public Law 102-73 (Titles II and III). This Act authorizes Federal funds for State-administered adult education programs with some national discretionary monies. States use a portion of their allocations under Section 353 of the Act to fund activities for family literacy and intergenerational programs. This section requires States to set aside at least 15 percent of their Federal grant for development of innovative and coordinated approaches in the delivery of adult education services through demonstration and teacher training special projects. Ten percent must be used for teacher training. States also use funds under Section 322 of the Act to help implement educational programs for families.	FY 93 Funds: $255	Ronald Pugsley, Acting Director Division of Adult Education and Literacy/ED 400 Maryland Ave. S.W. Washington, D.C. 20202-7240 (202) 205-8270
Library Services and Construction Act (Title I and VI) The Library Literacy Program provides grants to State and local public libraries for the support of literacy programs. Grant funds are used to coordinate and plan library literacy programs, to arrange training of librarians and volunteers to carry out these programs, for use of facilities, for dissemination and for acquiring literacy materials designed to improve the literacy levels of illiterate and functionally illiterate adults. Thirty-two percent of last year's grant awards were in the area of intergenerational literacy programs.	FY 93 Funds: $16.8 Million	Ray Fry, Director Library Literacy Programs Office of Educational Research and Improvement/ED (OERI) 555 New Jersey Ave. N.W. Washington, D.C. 20206 (202) 219-2293
Head Start Act The Head Start program is administered by the Administration for Children and Families (ACF) Department of Health and Human Services Regional Offices and the Indian and Migrant Program Branches. Grants are awarded to local public library systems for the purpose of operating Head Start programs at the community level. The programs are required to use non-Head Start resources in their communities for implementing programs for children and their parents.	FY 93 Funds: $2.7 Billion	Marlys Gustafson, Director Division of Program Development Administration for Children and Families Department of Health and Human Services Washington, D.C. 20201-0001 (202) 205-8578

FEDERAL LEGISLATION	FUNDING	CONTACT
Family Support Act of 1988 (Title IV-A), JOBS (Job Opportunities and Basic Skills Training Program) JOBS, a formula grant to States, provides Aid to Families with Dependent Children (AFDC) recipients with the opportunity to take part in education, job training and work activities. JOBS policies require coordination of new services with existing education program and job training. The program also requires efficient coordination between Federal, State and local governments in program design and administration.	FY 93 Funds: $1.6 Billion	Yvonne Howard, JOBS Coordinator Family Support Administration/HHS 370 L'Enfant Promenade, S.W. Washington, D.C. 20477 (202) 401-4619
Elementary and Secondary Education Act, as amended, Chapter I (Title I), Even Start Family Literacy Program Even Start is administered under Chapter I, Part B of the Act. Its purpose is to improve the educational opportunities of the nation's children and adults by integrating early childhood education and adult education for parents into a unified program. The agencies through cooperative projects that build on existing community resources to create a new range of services. Even Start became a State formula grant program in July 1992 when the appropriation exceeded over $50 million.	FY 93 Funds: 89.2 Million	Mary Jean Le Tendre, Director Compensatory Education Programs/ED 400 Maryland Avenue, S.W. Washington, D.C 20202 (202) 401-1682
Elementary and Secondary Education Act (Title VII, Bilingual Education The Family English Literacy Program (FELP) purpose is to provide families with limited English proficiency the opportunity to improve their literacy skills and behaviors. Under this discretionary program, funds are allocated to implement intergenerational literacy activities which may include language instruction, survival skills, and parenting skills.	FY 93 Funds: 6.2 Million	Mary Mahony, Project Officer Office of the Director for Bilingual Education and Minority Languages Affairs/ED 400 Maryland Ave. S.W. Washington, D.C. 202002 (202) 205-8728
Elementary and Secondary Education Act (Title III, Part B), Family School Partnership Program. The Fund for the Improvement and Reform of Schools and Teaching Act, as amended in 1988. The Family School Partnership Program provides assistance to local educational agencies eligible to receive grants under Chapter I of the Elementary and Secondary Education Act (ESEA), as amended to conduct projects that increase the involvement of families in improving educational achievement of their children. Discretionary funds are provided to projects for up to 36 months. Part C calls for the applicant to build on existing innovative family involvement programs in order to further develop, and evaluate, and disseminate these programs.	FY 93 Funds: $3.8 Million	Bryan Gray, Program Officer Fund for the Improvement and Reform of Schools and Teaching/ED (OERI) 555 New Jersey Ave. N.W. Room 522 Washington, D.C. 20206 (202) 219-1496

(Source: Scibles, 1993)

APPENDIX E

DIRECTORY OF LITERACY ORGANIZATIONS AND RESOURCES

American Association for Adult and Continuing Education (AAACE)
1112 Sixteenth St. NW Suite 420
Washington, DC 20036
(202) 463-6333

American Bar Association (ABA)
Task Force on Literacy
1800 M Street, NW
Washington, DC 20036
(202) 331-2287

American Library Association (ALA)
Office for Library Outreach Services
50 East Huron St.
Chicago, IL 606011
(312) 944-6780
1-800-545-2433

American Newspaper Publishers Association (ANPA) Foundation
Box 17407 Dulles Airport
Washington, DC 20041
(703) 648-1000

Barbara Bush Foundation for Family Literary
1002 Wisconsin Ave. NW
Washington, DC 20007
(202) 338-2006

Contact Literacy Center
P.O. Box 81826
Lincoln, NE 63501-1826
(402) 464-0602
1-800-228-8813

Correctional Education Association (CEA)
8025 Laurel Lakes Court
Laurel, MD 20707
(301) 490-1440

Education Commission of the States (ECS)
707 17th St. Suite 2700
Denver, CO 80202-3427
(303) 299-3600

ERIC
Clearinghouse on Adult Career and Vocational Education
1960 Kenny Road
Columbus, OH 43210
(614)486-3655

Illinois Literacy Resource Development Center
269 W. Clark St.
Champaign, IL 61820
(217) 355-6068

Institute for the Study of Adult Literacy
Penn State University
College of Education
248 Calder Way Suite 307
University Park, PA 16801
(814) 863-3777

International Reading Association (IRA)
800 Barksdale Rd.
P.O. Box 8139
Newark, DE 19714-8139
(302) 731-1600

Laubach Literacy Action (LLA)
1320 Jamesville Ave. Box 131
Syracuse, NY 13210
(315) 422-9121

Literacy Network, Inc.
475 Cleveland
St. Paul, MN 55104
(612) 646-5070

Literacy Volunteers of America, Inc. (LVA)
5795 Widewaters Parkway
Syracuse, NY 13214
(315) 445-8000

National Center for Family Literacy
Waterfront Plaza, Suite 200
325 W. Main St.
Louisville, KY 40402
(502) 584-1133

National Governor's Association (NGA)
444 North Capitol St. Suite 250
Washington, DC 20001
(202) 624-5300

National Institute for Literacy
800 Connecticut Ave. NW Suite 200
Washington, DC 20006
(202) 632-1500

Project Literacy U.S. (PLUS)
WQED
4802 Fifth Ave.
Pittsburgh, PA 15213
(412) 622-1300

Reading is Fundamental, Inc.
600 Maryland Ave. SW Suite 600
Smithsonian Institution
Washington, DC 20024-2520
(202) 287-3220

United Way of America
Community Initiatives Division
701 North Fairfax Street
Alexandria, VA 22314-2045

BIBLIOGRAPHY

Note: Starred items (*) are appropriate for use with beginning readers.

A Selected Family Literacy Resource Collection for Parents and Teachers

Arnold, Lois. *Preparing Young Children for Science, A Book of Activities.* New York: Schocken Books, 1980.

> A variety of activities designed to present science material to children using materials which are easily found in the home environment.

Barton, Bob. *Tell Me Another. (Storytelling and Reading Aloud at Home, at School and in the Community.)* Portsmouth, NH: Heinemann Educational Books, 1986.

> How to select, make up, and read stories to children.

Biagi, Bob. *Working Together: A Manual for Helping Groups Work More Effectively, Citizen Training Project.* Amherst, MA: University of Massachusetts, 1978.

Board of Cooperative Education *Two Hundred Ways to Help Children Learn.* Reston, VA: Reston Publishing Co., 1976.

> A collection of games, activities, and suggestions for preschool children which can be used at home or school.

Bogehold, Betty. *Getting Ready to Read.* New York: Bank Street College of Education, n.d.

The developmental stages of children from infancy to age six are linked with practical games, activities which will help lay the foundation for reading.

Brazelton, T. Berry. *To Listen to a Child: Understanding the Normal Problems of Growing Up.* Reading, MA: Addison-Wesley, 1984.

The noted Harvard pediatrician explores common childhood issues from the point of view of both the child and his or her parent.

*Bringing Up our Children. Billerica, MA: Curriculum Associates, 1991.

A series of easy-to-read articles on family issues designed to promote literacy within the family.

Broad, Laura Peabody. *The Playgroup Handbook.* New York: St. Martin's Press, 1974.

Developed by two playgroup mothers, includes both seasonal and non-seasonal activities arts and crafts, cooking, games, music, exercise in concise easy to read style.

Brown, Sam Ed. *One, Two Buckle My Shoe. (Math Activities for Young Children).* Mt. Ranier, MD: Gryphon Press, 1982.

Simple games which parents and teachers can follow develop math experience in such content areas as counting, matching, measurement, shapes, sequencing, estimation, and future planning. Also by the same author: *Bubbles, Rainbows and Worms: Science Experiments for Preschool children.*

Butler, Dorothy. *Babies Need Books.* New York: Athenaeum, 1982.

Books should play a prominent part in children's lives from babyhood on. A teacher (who is also a parent) presents a sequence of recommended books and activities from babyhood through age six for parents to use with their children.

Butler, Dorothy. *Cushla and Her Books.* Boston: Horn Book Inc., n.d.

The true story of the remarkable effect of books on the development of a multihandicapped child.

Butler, Dorothy and Marie Clay. *Reading Begins at Home.* Portsmouth, NH: Heinemann Educational Books, 1982.

Practical, workable activities that parents can provide for children to foster prereading activities.

Calendar of Home Activities. Billerica, MA: Curriculum Associates, 1991.

>A full year of daily activities for parents and children to complete at home. Calendars are effective September-August of each year.

Clay, Marie. *Writing Begins at Home: Preparing Children for Writing Before They Go to School.* Portsmouth, NH: Heinemann Books, 1987.

Cohen, Dorothy. *The Learning Child: Guidelines for Parents and Teachers.* New York: Schoken Books, 1972.

>A classic in developmental psychology of children, the author who taught at the Bank Street College of Education explores the successive stages of child development and demonstrates how parents and teachers can support a learning environment.

Cole, Ann, et al. *I Saw a Purple Cow (And 100 Other Recipes for Learning).* Boston, MA: Little Brown, 1981.

>A how-to book which encourages learning by doing; one-on-one and group activities which emphasize sharing between parent and child and support such important learning concepts as problem solving, reading/math skill building, and language development. Also by the same authors: *Purple Cow to the Rescue.*

Cowsill, Virginia. *Favorite Childhood Tales.* Syracuse, NY: New Reader's Press, 1990.

>Four childhood tales written down for beginning adult learners to share with their children.

Dixler, Debby. *Crayons, Crafts and Concepts.* Bridgeport, CT: First Teacher Books, n.d.

>Art activities organized around conceptual and theme areas which foster prereading skill development.

Evans, Judith. *Good Beginnings: Parenting in the Early Years.* Ypsilanti, MI: High Scope Press, 1982.

>In this practical manual, a developmental psychologist presents a variety of activities which parents can do and in terms they can understand during the seven stages from birth to 36 months.

Hearne, Betsy. *Choosing Books for Children: A Commonsense Guide.* New York: Dell, 1981.

>Selection of preschool books, easy reading for beginning readers and guidelines for choosing material for elementary school students around such areas as humor, poetry, mystery, etc.

*Holstein, Barbara B. *The Childbearing Years*. Syracuse, NY: New Reader's Press, 1991.

A chronicle of prenatal care for mothers-to-be with low reading skills.

Indenbaum, Valerie. *The Everything Book*. Mt. Ranier, MD: Gryphon House, 1983.

Activities designed to foster a positive self image and enjoyment of learning around monthly and seasonal themes. Included are: arts and crafts, stories, math, fingerplays, songs and books to support each theme.

Isenberg, Joan. *Playthings as Learning Tools: A Parents Guide*. New York: John Wiley, 1982.

Foster's development of children's language, thinking, and mathematical reasoning skills with an emphasis on children from three to seven.

*Keller, Roseanne. *When a Baby is New* and *As a Child Grows*. Syracuse, NY: New Reader's Press, 1990.

Written for new adult learners to learn more about child development. Also available in Spanish.

Kimmel, Margaret Mary. *For Reading Out Loud!* New York: Dell, 1983.

An introduction to the world of quality books, this features an annotated list of 140 read aloud titles for children from kindergarten to eighth grade. Also includes tips for reading aloud.

*Lewis, Barbara. *A New Beginning*. Syracuse, NY: New Reader's Press, 1990.

A month by month guide to the development of an infant written for adult new readers.

McCue, Lois. *Learning Through All Five Senses. (A Language Development Activity Book)*. Mt. Ranier, MD: Gryphon House, 1983.

The letters of the alphabet and phonetic sounds are taught through a series of activities which use all the five senses.

McMullan, Kate. *How to Choose Good Books for Kids*. Reading, MA: Addison Wesley, 1984.

An annotated booklist for preschool through middle school which helps parents select and motivate readers.

Marzollo, Jean and Janice Harper. *Learning Through Play*. New York, NY: Harper, 1974.

For parents or anyone who works with young children an inviting manual which presents topics, games and activities which teach learning through play.

*Push Literacy Action Now (PLAN). *Laying the Foundations: A Parent-Child Literacy Training Kit,* Washington, DC: n.d.

A training package for teachers and tutors working to develop parent-child curriculum with low literate parents. Accompanying video "From Crib to Classroom."

Reading Rainbow: A Guide for Teachers, Lincoln, NE: Programs 130. Great Plains Instructional Television, 1986.

Thirty of the popular Reading Rainbow (PBS series) books are presented with topics for discussion, activities and a supplementary booklist. An invaluable guide for parent or teacher.

Redleaf, Rhoda. *Open the Door, Let's Explore: Neighborhood Field Trips for Young Children.* Mount Rainer, MD: Toy's n' Things Press, 1983.

A comprehensive guide to activities designed to help children learn from neighborhood walks and field trips.

*Smith, Beverly. *The Long and Short of Mother Goose.* Syracuse, NY: New Reader's Press, 1990.

Sparling, Joseph and Isabelle Lewis. *Learning Games; For Threes and Fours.* New York: Walker and Co., 1984.

Over 100 games for preschoolers to do with their parents which help prepare children for following directions, answering questions, listening for letter sounds and getting ready to read.

Stetton, Mary. *Let's Play Science.* New York: Harper Colophon Books, 1979.

Easy science activities with simple pictures and large print. Simply presented and easy for beginning adult readers to use with children.

Trelease, Jim. *The New Read Aloud Handbook.* New York: Penguin Books, 1985.

A bestseller which promotes the importance of reading aloud to children for both parents and adults. Includes an annotated booklist of reading aloud favorites.

*Weinberg, Pamela. *Family Literacy and the School.* Syracuse, NY: New Reader's Press, 1990.

Written at a beginning reading level, this guide enables parents to understand the ways of communicating with schools.

Weinberg, Pamela. *Family Literacy and The School: How Teachers Can Help.* Syracuse, NY: New Reader's Press, 1990.

A guide for public school teachers and administrators to make them aware of parents of children who may have problems with reading and how to communicate with them.

Weinberg, Pamela. *Your Home is a Learning Place.* Syracuse, NY: New Readers Press, 1993.

"Low literate parents learn to teach basic skills at home."

SELECTED BROCHURES/BOOKLETS

American Library Association. "How to Raise a Reader: Sharing Books with Infants and Toddlers." Chicago, IL, 1990.

ALA/Bell Atlantic Family Literacy Project Fact Sheets:
"Libraries and Local Business Partnerships: Connections for Family Literacy"
"How to Start a Dial-A-Story"
"How to Recruit Participants Using Nonprint Media"
"Parenting Curriculum," (by Grace Cooper) includes the following titles:
"Getting to know your baby and yourself/prenatal to birth"
"Your New Human/Birth to One Month"
"Learning about the World/One to Three Months"
"Your Baby Grows/Three to Six Months"
"Learning More Each Day/ Six to Nine Months"
"The End of the First Year/Nine to Twelve Months"

Child Welfare League of America. Washington, D.C., 1973.

Six booklets designed for adolescent mothers which include child care and developmental information written at an easy reading level.

National Association for the Education of Young Children. Washington, D.C.

An outstanding catalog of monographs, books brochures, posters, and videotapes. For example:
"Toys, Tools for Learning " has a companion poster set.
McCracken, Janet Brown "Keeping Healthy: Parents, Teachers and Children."
McCracken, Janet Brown "Off to a Sound Start: Your Baby's First Year."
Schickedanz, Judith "Helping Children Learn about Reading."

Resources for Family Literacy and Community Collaboration Program Development

America 2000: An Education Strategy Sourcebook. Washington, DC: U.S. Department of Education, 1991.

Barbara Bush Foundation for Family Literacy. *First Teachers.* Washington, DC: Barbara Bush Foundation, 1989.

Beyond Rhetoric: A New American Agenda for Children and Families: Summary. Washington, DC: National Commission on Children, 1991.

Bruner, Charles. *Thinking Collaboratively: Ten Questions and Answers to Help Policy Makers Improve Children's Services.* Washington, DC: Education and Human Services Consortium, 1991

Clay, Marie M. *Observing Young Readers: Selected Papers.* Portsmouth, NH: Heinemann Books, 1982.

Confidentiality and Collaboration: Information Sharing in Interagency Efforts. A Joint Publication of Joining Forces, American Public Welfare Association and others. Denver, CO: Education Commission of the States Distribution Center, 1992.

Delgado-Gaitan, Concha. *Literacy for Empowerment.* Bristol, PA: Falmer Press, 1990.

Dickinson, David. *Bridges to Literacy: Approaches to Supporting Child and Family Literacy.* London: Basil Blackwell, (in press).

Edelman, Marion Wright. *Families in Crisis.* Cambridge, MA: Harvard University Press, 1987.

Edelman, Peter and Beryl A. Radin. *Serving Children and Families Effectively: How the Past Can Help the Future.* Washington, DC: Education and Human Services Consortium, 1992.

Edwards, Patricia. *Parent's as Partners in Reading: A Family Literacy Training Program.* Chicago, IL: Children's Press, 1990.

Evaluating Library Literacy Programs: A Manual for Reporting Accomplishments. Albany, NY: University of State of New York, State Department of Education, New York State Library, 1991.

Five Million Children: Our Nation's Poorest Citizens. New York: The National Center for Children in Poverty, Columbia University, 1991.

Goelman, Hillel, Antoinette Oberg, and Frank Smith. *Awakening to Literacy.* Portsmouth, NH: Heinemann Books, 1984.

Goldsmith, Ellen and Ruth Handel. *Family Reading: An Intergenerational Approach to Literacy.* Syracuse, NY: New Reader's Press, 1990.

Greene, Ellin. *Books Babies and Libraries: Serving Infants, Toddlers, Their Parents and Caregivers.* Chicago, IL: American Library Association, 1991.

Hall, Nigel. *The Emergence of Literacy.* Portsmouth, NH: Heinemann Books, 1987.

Habana-Hafner, Sally and Horace B. Reed & Assoc. *Partnerships for Community Development: Resources for Practitioners and Trainers.* Amherst, MA: University of Massachusetts (Center for Organizational and Community Development), 1989.

Heath, Shirley Brice. *Ways With Words: Language, Life and Work in Communities and Classrooms.* Cambridge, England: Cambridge University Press, 1983.

Himmelman, Arthur S. *Literacy Kit: Communities Working Collaboratively for a Change.* Alexandria, VA: United Way of America. Community Initiative Division, 1990.

Humes, Barbara and C. Cameron. *Library Literacy Program: Analysis of Funded Projects.* Washington, DC: Office of Educational Research and Improvement, U.S. Department of Education, 1990.

Illinois Literacy Resource Development Center. *The Mechanics of Success for Families: An Illinois Family Literacy Report.* Rantoul, IL: ILRDC, 1990.

Illinois Literacy Resource Development Center. *The Mechanics of Success for Families, Report #2, Evaluation.* Rantoul, IL: ILRDC, 1990.

Illinois Literacy Resource Development Center. *Fine Tuning the Mechanics of Success for Families, Report #3.*Rantoul, IL: ILRDC, 1991.

Illinois Literacy Resource Development Center. *Fine Tuning the Mechanics of Success for Families, Report #4.* Rantoul, IL: ILRDC, 1992.

Johnson, Debra Wilcox and Leslie Edmonds. *Family Literacy Library Programs: Models of Service.* Des Moines, IA: State Library of Iowa, 1990.

Kagan, Sharon et al. *America's Family Support Programs.* New Haven, CT: Yale University Press, 1987.

Kagan, Sharon L. *United We Stand: Collaboration for Child Care and Early Education Services.* New York: Teachers College Press, 1991.

Laminack, Lester. *Reading with Children Handbook.* Syracuse, NY: Literacy Volunteers of America, 1989.

Less Suffering, Less Fear: Meeting the Needs of America in the 90's: Report of the AJ Congress Task Force on the Unmet Needs of Low Income Households. New York: American Jewish Congress, 1991.

Levy, Janet E. and Carol Copple. *Joining Forces: A Report from the First Year.* Alexandria, VA: National Association of State Boards of Education, 1989.

Literacy Volunteers of America. *How to Start a Family Literacy Project.* Syracuse, NY: Literacy Volunteers of America, 1991.

McCracken, Robert and Marlene McCracken. *Stories, Songs and Poetry to Teach Reading and Writing.* (Literacy through Language). Chicago, IL: American Library Association, 1986.

McGee, Lea M. and Donald J. Richgels. *Literacy's Beginnings: Supporting Young Readers and Writers.* Boston: Allyn and Bacon, 1990.

McIvor, Conlan, ed. *Family Literacy in Action: A Survey of Successful Programs.* Syracuse, NY: New Reader's Press, 1990.

Melaville, Atelia and Martin Blank. *Together We Can: A Guide for Crafting a Profamily System of Education and Human Services.* Washington, D.C.: U.S. Department of Education, 1993.

Monsour, Margaret and Carole Talan. *Library-Based Family Literacy Projects.* Chicago, IL: American Library Association, 1993.

Nash, Andrea. *English Family Literacy: An Annotated Bibliography.* Boston: English Family Literacy Project, University of Massachusetts, 1987.

National Center for Family Literacy. *A Guide to Funding Sources.* Louisville, KY, 1991.

National School Boards Association. *Link Up: A Resource Directory, Interagency Collaborations to Help Students Achieve.* Alexandria, VA, 1991.

National Voluntary Health and Social Welfare Organization. *Community Collaboration Manual.* Washington, DC, 1990.

Nickse, Ruth S. *Family and Intergenerational Literacy Programs: An Update of "The Noises of Literacy."* Columbus, OH: ERIC Clearinghouse on Adult, Career and Vocational Education. Ohio State University, 1990.

Reading is Fundamental, Inc. *Family Literacy: Eight Model Programs from Reading is Fundamental.* Washington, DC, 1990.

Rockefeller Foundation. *Literacy and the Marketplace: Improving the Literacy of Low-Income Single Mothers.* New York, 1989.

SCANS Blueprint for Community Action: Building Community Coalitions. Washington, DC: Secretary's Commission on Achieving Necessary Skills (SCANS). U.S. Department of Labor, 1991.

Schorr, Lisbeth. *Within Our Reach: Breaking the Cycle of Disadvantage.* New York: Doubleday, 1988.

Schrage, Michael. *Shared Minds: The New Technologies of Collaboration.* New York: Random House, 1990.

Smith, R.C. and others. *Let's Do It Our Way: Working Together for Educational Excellence (A Handbook for School Community Collaboration).* Chapel Hill, NC: MDC, Inc., 1991.

Sticht, Thomas and Barbara McDonald. *The Intergenerational Transfer of Cognitive Ability.* Vols. I & II. Norwood, NJ: Ablex, 1991.

Solorzano, Ronald W., Ph.D and Reynaldo Baca. *An Evaluation of California's Families for Literacy Program.* Pasadena, CA: Educational Testing Service, Southern California Field Office, 1991.

Taylor, Denny. *Family Literacy: Young Children Learning to Read and Write.* Portsmouth, NH: Heinemann Educational Books, 1983.

Taylor, Denny and Dorothy Strickland. *Family Storybook Reading.* Portsmouth, NH: Heinemann Educational Books, 1986.

What it takes: Structuring Interagency Partnerships to Connect Children and Families with Comprehensive Services. Washington, DC: Education and Human Services Consortium, 1991.

Weiss, Heather B. and Francine H. Jacobs, eds. *Evaluating Family Programs.* New York: Aldine de Gruyter, 1988.

Youth Indicators, 1991: Trends in the Well-Being of American Youth. Washington, DC: U.S. Department of Education. Office of Educational Research and Improvement, 1991.

AUDIO/VIDEO

Bridge to Community: Providence Public Library's Family Literacy Program, 1991-92. Providence Public Library, Providence, RI.

Describes the Providence Public Library's collaboration with community agencies. Useful to help tutors and learners raise awareness of the issue of family literacy.

Close to Home: Library-Based Family Literacy. Towson, MD. ALA Video/Library Video Network, 1992.

Family Reading: An Intergenerational Approach to Literacy. Training Video. Syracuse, NY: New Reader's Press, 1990.

Families for Literacy. Carole Talan, Executive Producer. California State Library, Sacramento, CA. 1992.

First Things First. Pittsburgh, PA: WQED, 1990.

For Sam's Sake. Pasadena Public Library, Los Angeles, 1990.

From Crib to Classroom. Washington, DC. Push Literacy Action Now (PLAN), 1990.

Getting Others Involved in Children's Education. Pittsburgh, PA: WQED, n.d.

Parents and Children Together. Bloomington, IN: Family Literacy Center at Indiana University. (Monthly audio journal which encourages parents to read to their children.)

Project Lifelong Learning. Pittsburgh, PA: The Institute for the Study of Adult Literacy at Penn State/WQED/Pittsburgh and PLUS (Project Literacy U.S), 1992.

Three videos on family literacy, the community and the workplace with support materials in print for community leaders, administrators, and teachers.

Read to Me. Barksdale, MD: Idaho Literacy Project Video (Distributed by the International Reading Association), 1991.

Reading to Your Children. Billerica, MA: Curriculum Associates, 1991.

Reading with Children: Training Module. Syracuse, NY: Literacy Volunteers of America, 1989.

INDEX

Name Index

Shelley Quezada is Consultant, Library Services for the Unserved, Commonwealth of Massachusetts, Board of Library Commissioners, and lecturer in Adult and Family Literacy, Simmons College, Graduate School of Library and Information Science.

Ruth S. Nickse, Ph.D., President of Nickse Associates, is a distinguished researcher, speaker, writer, and consultant with more than twenty years' of experience in adult basic education. For the past five years she has consulted with Abt Associates, Inc. as a member of the research team on the national evaluation of Even Start, the Federal family literacy initiative.